Lighting the Way

The case for ethical leadership in schools

Angela Browne

BLOOMSBURY EDUCATION

LONDON OXFORD NEW YORK NEW DELHI SYDNEY

BLOOMSBURY EDUCATION
Bloomsbury Publishing Plc
50 Bedford Square, London, WC1B 3DP, UK

BLOOMSBURY, BLOOMSBURY EDUCATION and the Diana logo are trademarks of
Bloomsbury Publishing Plc

First published in Great Britain, 2020

ISBN: PB: 978-1-4729-7246-0; ePDF: 978-1-4729-7244-6; ePub: 978-1-4729-7245-3

2 4 6 8 10 9 7 5 3 1 (paperback)

Typeset by Newgen KnowledgeWorks Pvt. Ltd., Chennai, India
Printed and bound by CPI Group (UK) Ltd, Croydon, CR0 4YY

To find out more about our authors and books visit www.bloomsbury.com
and sign up for our newsletters

Contents

Acknowledgements

There are so many people behind the scenes of successful school leadership and most of them don't work in schools! There are also a huge number of people I have worked with across a range of schools who have helped me to find the words for this book, through their pushback, through their openness and often through voicing their frustrations.

I would like to express particular thanks to the following people:

Kerri ní Dochartaigh and Anna Willis, and Katie Sobol, Will Roberts, James Pope, Lisa Howell and David Spence, dear colleagues and friends through whom I have learned an immense amount about myself as a school leader.

Hannah Wilson and the WomenEd team, who over the past few years have helped me find my voice, encouraged me to share that voice and introduced me to a network of powerhouses, people all wanting to nudge the system towards change.

Helen Diamond and Hannah Marston at Bloomsbury, who ran with this idea for a book and who have championed the work throughout.

Most importantly, though, I want to acknowledge and thank Ivo and Arthur, who have been the steady background to my work in education. It is through their compassion, kindness and support that this is possible.

Introduction

The title of this book is inspired by the authors and communications experts Nancy Duarte and Patti Sanchez. In their book, *Illuminate*, they set out a captivating description of what it means to be a leader, as they depict leaders as those who 'patrol the border' between what has been and what will be. They, the authors, explain that it is a leader's role to 'light the way' to a 'better reality' (Duarte and Sanchez, 2016).

That said, the genesis for this book came many years ago and well before I was a headteacher. It came during my time as a teacher and senior leader, when watching the many ways the school system failed to adequately support some of our most vulnerable students. Around that time, I began to talk about the 'nourished school', an idea that acted as an umbrella for all the things I thought the school system needed to take more care to incorporate.

The pillars of the nourished school, I believed, were 'nourishment' through healthy food, a focus on the 'spiritual dimension' of the human being, 'time spent in nature' and the 'development of a craft'. These elements I saw as foundational and as contributory to the successful development of young people.

Most of the books I had read while I was a trainee teacher had been about curriculum and pedagogy. Naturally, as I progressed through school leadership, I began to read books about how one should lead a school and the skills, knowledge and understanding one should possess. The thing is that many of these books didn't meet me where I was. I often felt awed, flawed and a bit crumpled when I read these books of school leadership success and I began to feel that I wanted to set out a counter narrative to leadership.

Time passed and I realised that many of my ideas had been naïve. The pressures of leading a school through financial difficulty led me to conclude that the pillars of the nourished school could never make it onto a headteacher's list of priorities. Nevertheless, the call to enact and articulate a counter narrative remained. I felt there was a compelling narrative to tell of what school leadership could be, and my ideas and behaviours began to coalesce around this.

In 2017, the multi-academy trust I worked for was invited to take part in a BBC documentary series called *School*. Our work as a trust and my role as acting headteacher in one of the schools were captured through the lens over a school year.

I was keen to take part in the programme because I believed that, in demonstrating some of the challenges and in being open about them, it could help to normalise experiences for other educators and shine a light on just how difficult life in many schools had become. I also wanted to light a way towards ethical leadership in the face of these challenges.

What the programme did was to depict an education system on the edge of crisis, with staff and students burning out and more importantly a system failing to fulfil its role as what could be considered the fourth emergency service. Responses to the series underscored the resonance of the issues the programme highlighted.

My part in the series was relatively brief but what I hope I demonstrated was that school leaders, now more so than ever, need to be prepared to lead in the face of social turmoil, need to be prepared to be torchbearers and to light the way to a new and as yet unimagined reality. Schools need leaders who are unafraid of the dissolution of the institution and who are prepared to face the disintegration of all that is not working with optimism and faith in renewal.

After the series was aired, the themes for this book emerged with greater clarity and I set about writing *Lighting the Way*, a book for the ordinary school leader who tries and sometimes fails, but who then tries a bit more. This book is for those who, lost in the nuances of their context, are not looking for the 'right' way but are looking for the courage to forge 'their way'. This book is for the thousands of everyday headteachers who are just trying to get it right and who know that the time is coming when something must give or completely change.

In this book, I have attempted to light a way for school leaders in need of encouragement and support towards ethical action and to light a way for new leaders who are keen to do things differently. I make no judgments about leaders who are leading in the tried and true ways of the educational establishment but rather I attempt to carve a space for an alternative model of school leadership that places ethical action, compassion, knowledge of self and a commitment to human flourishing at its core.

PART 1

The case for school leadership

1 Communities in crisis

Chapter overview

This chapter considers the extent to which the communities that many schools serve are in crisis. It looks at the recent past in which, when families or children were in crisis, there was a hope of supporting them, providing signposting or helping in some way, and considers the current reality: times in which poverty is prevalent and pervasive. Why? Because to light the way we need to understand the current position and start to envision a brighter future.

I qualified as a teacher in 2001, taking my first job in an inner-city school in Bristol. The school drew from a wide range of ethnic minority groups and was located in what, for generations, had been a working-class community with Victorian housing stock designed originally for miners and mill workers, latterly peppered in the 1950s with the first high rises to be built outside of London.

The arrival of high numbers of asylum-seeking Somalis fleeing civil war, as part of the diaspora settling into this area of Bristol, meant that in the three or so years preceding my arrival at the school there had been a focus on services that could support families in crisis, as well as the need for integration. This meant that our school in particular was a place in which numerous funding streams converged.

This area of the city fell into the first round of communities benefitting from Tony Blair's New Deal for Communities regeneration programme. This was a programme designed to tackle the impact of poverty in 22 of the most deprived wards in the country. One of the benefits, and sometimes challenges, of working in a school transformed by the diaspora was that there were a number of children who spoke English as an additional language (EAL). For these children, additional funding made it possible for us to fund extra-curricular sessions targeted at supporting English language acquisition in order that our recently arrived children could make progress in line with their peers.

Additional funding for students with EAL made a huge difference. As an English teacher, there was very much a sense that you were supported by skilled practitioners experienced in harnessing the aptitude for language learning of many children. Indeed, the two-way flow of communication between the English department and the ESOL (English for Speakers of Other Languages) team was a critical factor in developing a rich understanding of the cultures, diversity and richness of our school.

The funding available at the time did not stop there. Parents of students who had EAL were also able to attend classes in English and basic skills to ensure that they would be able to fully participate in their local community, would be able to fully access the services they were entitled to and would be able to more fully support their children with their studies.

Between 2001 and 2003, 500 million pounds was poured into the Excellence in Cities programme that had been established by the Labour government to promote inclusion in the inner cities and tackle the chronic underachievement of many children. Under this programme, learning mentors were introduced to schools, and with this funding, schools were better able to set up specialist learning support units within their communities to support their more vulnerable children.

In our school we were able to use resources to both employ learning mentors and set up a specialist learning support unit. Indeed, so rich were the opportunities for funding that we were successful in bidding to open a provision purely for children at risk of exclusion on our school site. This pot of funding came from a youth charity but again was aimed at supporting the most vulnerable children and consequently their families.

Children who were identified as being in need of more support were given an allocation of time during the school day to work with trained colleagues. The provision for those children who had behavioural needs ran alongside the provision for children who had special educational needs. Again, our school was relatively time- and resource-rich (although even back then it didn't feel it). We had a school nurse, a school counsellor, a dyslexia teacher, a special educational needs and disabilities coordinator (SENDCo) and a deputy SENDCo, as well as numerous learning support assistants within the team.

New Labour had also committed to Sure Start Centres and, between 1991 and 2002, 452 million pounds was allocated to these centres, which were designed to provide integrated learning and childcare five days per week in the most deprived areas, along with family support and parenting advice, as well as access to specialist targeted advice.

As an assistant head overseeing an inclusion brief, I always felt that if I didn't have the answers, help would be at hand. Following the death of Victoria Climbié (who was murdered by her aunt and her aunt's boyfriend after suffering months of abuse, despite repeated contact with social services, the police and the NHS), schools, social services, child and adolescent mental health services (CAMHS) and health services that supported children and families had been quite rightly directed through the Every Child Matters agenda. The idea was that they would work more effectively together to safeguard children and ensure that no one slipped through the net. Yes, we all thought wryly, of course every child matters, and there was a sense that we were being taught to suck eggs, but this agenda meant that a new approach to multi-disciplinary working was set into motion, and the attention to rallying around families to ensure that the best possible support was being offered was palpable.

I remember multi-agency meetings in which every dimension of a family's support network was represented. Meetings in which one sometimes felt the overwhelm that the family must be experiencing as the multi-disciplinary army of colleagues were squeezed into a room to jointly action plan, signpost and agree resources and strategies to support them.

I remember a thick booklet detailing the support services available for vulnerable children or families in crisis. It was like a phone directory of support, with a paragraph per charity or agency explaining what they could do to be of service. Little did I know that, just a decade later, the comfort I felt in reaching for that booklet would be replaced with the desperate feeling that I had no answers, nothing to offer this family coming in to meet with me and no solution to mitigate the crushing reality of poverty, depression or difficult life circumstances they faced.

Today things feel markedly different in schools and, as the focus on high-profile cases of abuse and neglect has led policy and practice towards greater protection of children at risk and vulnerable families in need, so too has come a rise in the number of children in these categories. In 2017, the Children's Commissioner estimated that '670,000 English children live in "high-risk" situations, including with parents addicted to alcohol or drugs or in temporary accommodation, at least 800,000 have mental health disorders and 580,000 are in need of direct intervention' (Crenna-Jennings, 2018). Although between 2010 and 2016 the rate of all children in need per 100,000 decreased by one per cent, the rate of children issued with child protection plans rose, as did the rate of looked-after children.

The impact of poverty

These statistics are somewhat unsurprising, as the knock-on effects of poverty have a bearing. According to the report 'Vulnerable Children and Social Care in

England', the relationship between poverty and social care involvement is strong. '30 per cent of school-age children in mainstream provision on child in need plans and 37 per cent of those on child protection plans live in areas of high deprivation (based on IDACI bands), compared to 18 per cent of other children and 17 per cent of looked after children.' (Crenna-Jennings, 2018)

The 2018 annual Joseph Rowntree Foundation Report on poverty in the UK revealed that child poverty has been rising since 2011–12 and that 4.1 million children are now living in poverty, an increase of 500,000 in that time. The same report revealed that workers are now increasingly living in poverty and that 'in-work poverty has been rising faster than employment, driven almost entirely by increasing poverty among working parents'. The report continues that 'virtually all this rise in child poverty has taken place within working families. In the last five years, poverty rates have been rising for all types of working families – whether they are lone-parent or couple families and regardless of the number of adults in work or whether they are part-time or full-time workers.'

Poverty reaches into the nooks and crannies of our schools; it is pervasive, unavoidable and distressing. And it is not just limited to the children and families we work with. Indeed, increasing numbers of teachers also find themselves living the dire reality of poverty in modern Britain.

The charity Education Support Partnership, which was founded in 1877 as the Teachers' Benevolent Fund, received 85 applications from education staff in need of financial assistance in April 2018. This was the highest number of monthly applications it had had in its 141-year history. An article in the *Guardian*, written in June 2018 (Ferguson, 2018), stated that this spike in applications represented a 157 per cent increase compared with the same month last year. It continued to explain that the charity had already had over 300 applications for financial support halfway through 2018 and was starting to use cash reserves to try to meet the demand of the applications received. In addition to financial support, the number of educators accessing the teacher helpline had also risen sharply. The Education Support Partnership dealt with 9,615 cases between April 2018 and March 2019, which represented a 28 per cent rise from 2017.

This rise in the working poor is worrying and yet it is not often spoken of. The research (Cribb et al., 2018) tells us that since 2002–03, average housing costs have risen four times faster for children in low-income families than for those in middle-income families and that for those in the latter group, housing costs have risen by 11 per cent. The forecast for low- to middle-income families is that they will be worse off in 2024 than they were in 2004, with 37 per cent of children forecast to be growing up in poverty by this point.

Across the country, food bank usage has been on the rise. The Trussell Trust (2019) state that 'Between 1 April 2018 and 31 March 2019, the Trussell Trust's food bank network distributed 1.6 million three-day emergency food supplies to people in crisis, a 19% increase on the previous year. More than half a million of these went to children.'

And we can see this in our schools. Watching the increasing numbers of children who have not eaten or do not know whether they will eat after school. Witnessing the stress and distress for parents caused when a teacher explains that a replacement pair of trousers will need to be bought. Witnessing the decline in the numbers of children able to go on school trips and visits. Knowing that conversations will inevitably lead back to what is unaffordable in a household when a parent comes in initially to talk on a different topic. These markers of poverty are ever present and they have been increasing but, like the frog becoming accustomed to the increasing water temperature, perhaps we have not truly realised the dire state we are in and the huge cost to our communities of poverty in modern Britain.

The wide gap in school performance

The effects of community disadvantage, as well as family disadvantage, begin well before children start school, and this effect can remain with them throughout their schooling (Social Mobility Commission, 2019). This means that for children in our classes who come from areas of persistent disadvantage (for example, the south-east of England, where chronic disadvantage has been a persistent feature of many communities and where childhood poverty reaches 50 per cent in some constituencies), their outlook is markedly different to non-disadvantaged children or those who have not grown up with this persistent history of poverty.

Growing up in poverty is more likely to have an impact on a child's physiological and physical health, on their wellbeing and on their ability to retain information and 'perform' under pressure. Before birth, a mother's perinatal health is already having a bearing. The research tells us that 'stress during pregnancy is linked to poorer foetal and cognitive development' (Crenna-Jennings, 2018). Crenna-Jennings continues that 'living in challenging social and economic conditions breeds chronic stress; analysis of UK-wide GP records found that the odds of deprived mothers aged 35 to 45 years experiencing antenatal depression or anxiety were more than two and a half times greater compared to non-deprived mothers.'

Breastfeeding has been strongly linked to positive cognitive development in children and yet in the UK we have one of the lowest rates of breastfeeding in the developed world. Rates of breastfeeding in the UK also differ in terms of social economics, with a greater prevalence found within women in managerial positions and with 15 per cent fewer women in routine or manual jobs breastfeeding their children (Crenna-Jennings, 2018).

The impact of smoking, alcohol and diet all contribute to maternal and early childhood health and, with the research telling us that 'expectant mothers living in deprived areas in the UK are substantially more likely to smoke [which has been] attributed to higher levels of stress associated with hardship and a lack of access to support' (Crenna-Jennings, 2018), clearly a child growing up in a house in which there is poverty is facing challenges very early on in life.

Adverse childhood experiences

In 1998, a doctor in San Diego collaborated with a doctor from the Center for Disease Control and Prevention in America to conduct the largest ever study on the impact of adverse childhood experiences (ACEs) and their impact on health later in life. The 17,000 participants in the study were largely middle-class, white, college-educated professionals and they were asked about the existence of physical abuse, sexual abuse, emotional abuse, physical neglect, emotional neglect, divorced parents, a parent in prison, mental illness, substance abuse or domestic violence in their childhood. The results were profound. What became clear to the researchers was that the prevalence of ACEs was high; indeed, two in three adults had suffered from one or more ACEs. One in eight participants in the study had suffered four or more ACEs and, with this higher prevalence of trauma in their lives, were more likely to suffer from health problems or engage in risk-taking behaviours. The study (Centers for Disease Control and Prevention, 2019) found that those with six or more ACEs were likely to die an average of 20 years earlier than those without one.

A few years later, Dr Nadine Burke carried out similar research (Burke et al., 2011) with some of her patients in a socially deprived area of San Francisco. What was interesting was that, although the sample population was very different, the prevalence of ACEs was not. Again, in her community, two-thirds of the population had experienced one or more ACEs and one in eight had experienced four or more. What stands out from Burke's study is the correlation between ACEs and learning and behaviour in school. For those with four or more ACEs, there was a far greater prevalence of learning and behaviour issues in comparison to those with no ACEs (51.2 per cent as opposed to three per cent).

In the UK, Mark Bellis, across two studies, one in 2014 and one in 2015, found that nearly 50 per cent of the population had experienced one or more ACE, that in England eight per cent of the population had experienced four or more, and that in Wales that percentage rose to 14 per cent. A 2014 study identified people with four or more ACEs as being four times more likely to be high-risk drinkers, six times more likely to be smokers, 16 times more likely to be crack cocaine or heroin users, 15 times more likely to have been involved in violence over the past year and 20 times more likely to be in prison during their lifetimes (Bellis et al., 2014).

The intergenerational nature of ACEs makes the jobs of schools and educators more nuanced, and the cross-population reach of them means that every teacher is working with crisis to some degree. From private schools to schools in areas of multiple deprivation, the impact of ACEs is profound.

That said, there is compelling evidence that the community within which a child grows up will have a significant impact on their outcomes. In a study undertaken by Chetty, Hendren and Katz (2016), the researchers reviewed the outcomes of the 'Moving to Opportunity' programme, a scheme in which participants were given vouchers to help them move from deprived housing projects to social housing in more affluent areas. Previous studies had demonstrated that the programme had an impact on the health and wellbeing of participants but there had been no evidence that it had a bearing on participants' ability to obtain better earning potential. However, they found that, to the contrary, 'children who moved to lower-poverty areas when they were young [were] more likely to attend college and have substantially higher incomes as adults'.

The panacea for all social ills

In her wide-ranging speech at the launch of Ofsted's 2017–18 Annual Report, Amanda Spielman explained her view that schools should not be the panacea for all of society's ills (Spielman, 2018). While I understand that position, she gave the example of children coming to school aged four still wearing nappies or pull-ups. This, she said, was a disruptive factor for teachers and other children, as schools were now having to deal with issues that should be being dealt with by parents. Spielman also talked about knife crime in that speech, explaining that while schools do have a role in educating children on the dangers of knife crime, they can't actually take on this problem for themselves, even if crime creeps up to the edges of what is happening in school. And finally, she gave the example of the obesity crisis, stating that schools that try to tackle issues such as rising obesity levels with children and families are in fact making no greater in-roads than schools that don't tackle these issues at all.

I take this point; I agree that there can be an over-involvement on our part as educators, particularly with issues that feel as though they are hampering our ability to do our day-to-day work. However, isn't it also the case that we cannot truly disassociate ourselves with society's ills when education has become, as Spielman acknowledged, a frontline service? The fact is that the context in which children are growing up has a huge bearing on the ways we are able to support and work with them. I really do not believe these things can be separated, nor should they be.

So, while we cannot be a panacea, there seems to be a responsibility to shift ourselves and bend ourselves according to the times we find ourselves in. We are no longer just providers of education; indeed there is an expectation that as professionals we take on a new level of responsibility. In fact, I think there is an expectation foisted upon us by parents and I understand why. Because generally there is an absence of leadership. There are no community leaders, church attendance is down, there are no community spaces, there are few shared free services, and there is little in the way of mentoring, advice or advocacy. There's barely anything left.

I think it is incumbent upon us to turn our heads towards the most pressing of society's ills, line ourselves up with them and try to work with them. This means that we need to understand poverty and we need to understand the impact of poverty, not just on the attainment gap but on all aspects of childhood. We need to be able to accept our role in supporting families because without this the impact of education on a child's life will never be fully realised.

This work requires a new style of leadership and, as this book will explore, it requires the kind of leadership that asks us to look into ourselves and determine where we stand in the world and what our beliefs and values are. If, as school leaders, we believe that we should not participate in the realm of social transformation, if we believe that children can come into our schools and drop their context at the school gate, and if we believe we are just filling their heads with knowledge and sending them out into the world, then we are really failing to engage with our leadership potential.

Given the scale of the crisis we are witnessing, the school as a standalone institution is not, in my opinion, a responsible place to reside. Too many children today are growing up in dire circumstances and so schools must work together with other agencies and organisations to do everything they can to alleviate some of the difficulty. This means that schools must be outward facing and must develop an assuredness in their ability to manage a broad range of challenges and issues that exist as part of life in modern Britain.

Key questions to help you light the way

1. What are the challenges that poverty brings to your school or community?
2. How does your school manage the challenges of poverty?
3. How well attuned is your school to the experiences of families in poverty?
4. How successfully is your school addressing the poverty gap?
5. How comfortable does your leadership team feel about your school being a panacea for many societal ills?
6. What is your vision for our society? How can you light the way?

2 A system on the brink

Chapter overview

This chapter considers the extent to which we are witnessing an education system on the brink of dissolution. It considers the combined and sometimes opposing forces of decentralisation coupled with scrutiny and accountability, as well as the impact of high-stakes accountability systems. Finally, this chapter will explore some of the bright spots and grassroots movements that have emerged out of this system on the edge. Why? Because to light the way we need to understand the current reality within education and begin to articulate, if only in our minds, how and why it must change.

A brief history of post-war education reform

It was the Education Act of 1944 that led to a state education that looks pretty much as we know it today. The compulsory school age was raised to 15 and the Act created free state education and separated out primary schools from secondary schools. It also gave responsibility to local education authorities to provide nurseries and for children who had special educational needs. Although the principle of free education for all was established in the Act, there was a division between schools into grammar, secondary modern and sometimes technical schools, so the idea that schools could exist for students with different types of mind or ability was established. Comprehensive schools were slowly emerging across the country during the period 1944 to 1976 but, as sociologist Stephen Ball (2017) explains in his book *The Education Debate*, 'change was slow and piecemeal and incoherent with little evidence of drastic reform'.

In 1976, James Callaghan, the Labour prime minister, gave a speech on the state of education. In many ways, it reads today as a speech that could be taken from recent months. He talks of girls abandoning science before leaving school. He talks about concerns over the standards of numeracy of school leavers. He continues to express concerns over deficiencies in the cooperation between schools and industry and wonders why there remain 30,000 vacancies for students in science and engineering in universities and polytechnics. In his speech, Callaghan also talks about what he describes as new, informal methods of teaching. These we would recognise today as more progressive approaches to teaching and learning; indeed, this debate around progressive and traditional approaches continues 40 years later on Twitter every day. Callaghan signals a move in his 1976 speech towards a basic curriculum with what he describes as having universal standards. He suggests that the balance has been wrong and that there is no virtue in producing 'socially well-adjusted members of society who are unemployed because they do not have skills'.

As Stephen Ball (2017) puts it, 'in a number of ways Callaghan's speech opened up a set of policy agendas that were vigorously pursued by the Conservative government of 1979 to 1997'. In other ways, this sense of teachers and schools being ungovernable and untouchable that is hinted towards in the Callaghan speech laid the groundwork for a more neoliberal approach to British politics and to education.

Margaret Thatcher's first education secretary, Mark Carlisle, was influenced by his advisor Stuart Sexton, who had contributed to the last set of Black Papers published in 1977. The Black Papers were a series of articles that had been published as an antidote to the government white papers of the time, and they set out a strong criticism of what they saw as the failures of a progressive education system that had gone too far. Carlisle felt strongly that there was a need to move away from post-war social welfare concerns and to embrace policies rooted in a freer market anti-statism. This model would see parents having choice over where their children went to school; it would see a regulated system in which there would be an independent inspectorate and 'minimum standards and a minimum curriculum' (Gillard, 2018).

What is described as 'a paradox at the very heart of the new right philosophy' is the combination of education policies that, as Gillard states, could be seen as examples of neoconservatism as well as manifestations of neoliberalism, exemplified by heavily enforced aspects of policy coming at the same time as increased freedoms. During Margaret Thatcher's tenure, in a neoconservative gesture, the National Curriculum was established and an accountability system was put in place, with Ofsted and Estyn being introduced. While at the same time neoliberalism was signalled, in that parents were given the right to choose a preference of state schools, there was a devolution of control of budgets from local authorities to schools, and information about poor schools or failing teachers became more readily available for the 'market'.

Under Tony Blair's New Labour from 1997, a 'Third Way' was articulated. New Labour, as we have explored in Chapter 1, made a flurry of systematic investments in education and committed ambitiously to education reform through numerous policies and initiatives. In many ways, Margaret Thatcher's neoliberalism was seen as being continued and expanded upon by Tony Blair's Third Way. As Stephen Ball (2017) explains, the Third Way did not look back 'to a pre-welfare market heyday [but] it was about moving on and was centred on the project of modernisation'. In the government white paper 'Excellence in schools' (Secretary of State for Education and Employment, 1997), the mix of state intervention and renewed freedoms was set out. Education would be at the heart of government, suggesting a deep interest in its direction and motivation. Policies would be designed to benefit the many, not just a few, gesturing towards a state moral authoritarianism that would proliferate and be explained through policies. Standards would matter more than structures in a nod towards continued inspection and accountabilities. Intervention would be in inverse proportion to success and there would be zero tolerance of underperformance. Here the heavy hand of accountability is signalled. And finally, the government would work in partnership with all those committed to raising standards, suggesting the deregulatory aspects of the system and the involvement of the market.

Much like the transition from a Conservative to a Labour government, the Labour to coalition government transition in 2010 did not see the outright rejection of previous education policies but rather saw the 'accretion and sedimentation' process continue (Ball, 2017). The coalition did not enact a clean-slate approach but rather built on the aspects of neoliberalism and neoconservatism to support their education policies. David Cameron's commitment in 2011 to 'mend our broken society' meant a focus on and a return to the values of a good education. The government talked of reinstalling all that had been 'good' about the post-1944 system of grammar schools, a traditional curriculum, physical discipline and exclusions. And as Stephen Ball explains, there was 'on the one hand... [a] neoconservative process of cultural restorationism' and on the other, 'as part of a neoliberal process of change', an encouragement for schools to act more like businesses and to become more enterprising (Ball, 2017).

A confusing paradox at the heart of schools

So, given the recent history of our education system, it is not surprising that we find ourselves in a situation where we feel increasingly accountable, and yet are told that we work in a system that is relatively deregulated and devolved. The way in which the language about education contains both neoliberal and neo-conservative terms adds to the confusion. Educators are increasingly familiar with targets, accountability, ideas around devolution, choice, performance-related pay, freedoms and so forth. Phrases like 'earned autonomy' abound in our sector and this is identified as what Paul Dugay, Professor of Sociology and Organization Studies, calls 'controlled decontrol': 'the use of devolution and autonomy as freedom is set within the constraints and requirements of performance and profitability' (Ball, 2017).

This paradox has been immensely damaging to the profession and it rumbles away alongside the deeper issue of schools as marketplaces – marketplaces in which knowledge is seen as a commodity that will ultimately further the progression of the nation, in which competition for children who will support the furtherance of the organisation is a factor and in which questions of finance abut uncomfortably with issues of ethics.

For many educators, what is unspoken but what exists incongruently is that we now have the 'freedom' to be accountable for running fiscally healthy organisations, the freedom to, however we see fit, lead schools in which the performance of students and staff is measured and is strong, and the freedom to compete in the sector, demonstrating quality in the marketplace. It could be argued, however, that these are not freedoms at all. Especially when the threat of what happens when people underperform is around every corner.

A workforce in crisis

There are daily stories in our papers about the challenges that new teachers face, and the retention of early career teachers bears this out. School workforce data identifies that the percentage of teachers remaining in the profession after their first year has dropped from around 87 per cent to 85 per cent. It goes on to evidence a three-year retention drop of 80 per cent to 73 per cent and a five-year retention drop from 73 per cent in 2011 to 67 per cent in 2017 (Worth, 2018).

For many new teachers, the shock of not being able to fulfil their ambitions of making a difference and supporting young people through delivering a subject they are passionate about is devastating. New teachers cite huge problems in managing the workload and attaining a work–life balance, as well as unease with a target-driven system. For others, seeing their contemporaries thrive in the private sector, in which higher pay and better working conditions prevail, is enough to have them packing their bags.

My experiences of leading in schools with new teachers has, at times, been heartbreaking. I've witnessed first-hand the excitement, the will to make it work, and the energies poured into planning, marking and supporting learning. I remember INSET days with fresh-faced new teachers excited by the community of the school and the support of peers, and I remember seeing the exhaustion soon set in – the understanding of the demands but the inability to be able to juggle it all. I saw in particular the degenerative effect on teachers of managing support for children who struggled in the classroom, trying to differentiate across an increasingly broad spectrum, and the difficulties of managing parents' demands. As the school year progressed, despite trying to pour more and more into supporting these teachers, the only true support was to give them the time they needed to explore whether or not this was the profession for them. Invariably it was not and, often with broken hearts, they wearily made their way off and out down a different path.

We also hear with regularity stories from experienced teachers for whom the pressure makes them feel that the job is no longer worth doing. The newspaper headlines speak volumes: 'Every lesson is a battle: why teachers are lining up to leave', 'Teachers experience more stress than other workers, study shows', 'Teachers risk dying in classrooms in illnesses ignored, union told', 'One in four teachers experience violence from pupils every week', 'One in five teachers using own money for school supplies'. It goes on and on. With statistics suggesting that one-fifth of teachers intend to leave the profession within two years and fewer teachers making it through to retirement, the overall opinion is that teaching is a profession that is simply not viable.

We hear that there is a shortage in the pipeline of leaders and headteachers, and this shortage is set against the weekly stories of headteachers losing their positions as a result of the incredibly high stakes that leadership in schools now carries. Official figures from the Department for Education show that almost a third of headteachers leave within three years of taking up the post. Unsurprisingly, much of this is linked to unfavourable Ofsted reports and the pressure this places on school leaders. In compiling the NFER report 'Keeping your head' (Lynch et al., 2017), 22 headteachers were interviewed and they suggested that the reasons for leaving the profession were 'system instability (the pace and nature of policy changes) and mixed experiences of support'.

The personal toll

As a headteacher, I am unashamed about describing the impact that the stress of high-stakes accountability has had on my life. I remember stress so intense that at times I wanted to drive my car off the road because the day spent in hospital with minor injuries would be more pleasant than a day spent in my school.

Regularly waking at two o'clock in the morning, three o'clock in the morning, four o'clock in the morning and failing to get back to sleep marked many of my days as a headteacher. Not knowing how to handle the complexities of school finance and limited school resources, along with the growing challenges of children who had special educational needs and disabilities marked my time as a headteacher. Knowing that I could not support effectively the number of teachers who were struggling under the weight of the impact of limited financial resources and children in their classes who had extreme and complex needs marked my time as a headteacher. Attending governors' meetings was enough to bring about illness, sadness and tears. I was lucky I had a supportive group of governors but the experience of regularly feeling an absolute failure was one that I have no desire to repeat.

My days and months were spent delivering bad news. Bad news to parents, to stakeholders, to staff. I went from the dizzying heights of personal and professional success to feeling so utterly useless in my inability to get it right, in my inability to make everything work, in my failure to keep complaints at bay, that I knew there was no option but to resign.

I believe that there has been a concerted effort to strip educators of their autonomy. This stripping away of autonomy has allowed the intertwining of the identities of teachers and school leaders with the identities of their schools.

When I left my second headship, it was almost impossible to separate my identity from that of the school. Furthermore, the accountability system and the means by which Ofsted talk about leadership in both generic and very specific terms meant that I felt that the school's success was my success, that the school's failure was my failure.

At the end of a relatively gruelling Ofsted, I felt my personal abilities, skills, knowledge, expertise and qualities to be under attack. I remember, in fact, one Ofsted inspector asking me on the morning of the second day, in such a peculiar way, whether or not I was OK. He had not been someone who had been on our side. He had made decisions about the quality of education, which he did not feel was satisfactory, before the end of the first morning.

I'm not in any way bitter about the experience of the majority of that Ofsted visit, but this one inspector – the way he approached me, sidling up and asking whether I was OK because 'this was a very difficult thing that I was going through' – now gives me a cause for concern. The school was not me; I was not the school. We had tried to set something up that would be an alternative to mainstream school provision. Some of what we had done had worked and some of it hadn't, but my identity as a woman, as a leader, as a parent, as a human being with agency, interests, experience and autonomy was not the school's identity.

I wonder about all of the leaders who have been ousted from failing schools. I wonder about their mental health. I wonder about their sense of self. I wonder about the extent to which the agenda to ensure that leaders feel that their identity is the school's identity has been part of a wider school improvement agenda. Not everyone wants to learn this lesson, and the terrible cost on individual headteachers as the axe falls following a set of results that are deemed unsatisfactory or the failure to improve a school at the expected rate is profound. The gnawing, nagging doubts that you will be next, you will be caught out, the axe will fall on you is ever present and, for those on whom the axe has already come down, they are left tainted with 'failure'. Picking themselves up and getting back out there is nothing short of heroic.

It wasn't until I returned to headship for the third time that I realised that it wasn't so much that I wasn't good enough but rather that the job wasn't doable enough. The system often made me feel that I was a failure. Sometimes it felt I couldn't move for hero headteachers to the left and right of me. However, what I learned from my third headship was that, paraphrasing Theodore Roosevelt (1910), being 'prepared to stand in the arena' was an exceptional feat. In other words, showing up every day, putting my head above the parapet and being prepared to lead through all the challenges that school leadership brings was good enough. I need not be any more heroic than that.

Bright spots

Luckily, it is not all doom and gloom. Indeed, I think it is important to salvage hope and recognise that there are many, many people working within the education sector who are determined to make things better in spite of the scale of the challenge. Thus, in the face of the growing crisis in the system, there have been sector-wide bright spots and evidence that alternative, fresh and inspiring voices can be heard on platforms that are being constructed within the grassroots.

WomenEd

In 2017, just two years after being created, WomedEd was shortlisted as an Outstanding Diversity Network at the National Diversity Awards. As Hannah Wilson describes in the opening chapter to WomenEd's book *10% Braver*, their public recognition came swiftly within two years, as they were 'invited to sit on a diversity roundtable chaired by schools minister Nick Gibb to consult on the department's diversity agenda and represented the voice of female teachers and leaders at the DFE summit on flexible working' (Porritt and Featherstone, 2019).

WomenEd was very much born in the face of the growing education crisis. Their mission is to empower more women in education to have the choice to progress on the leadership journey. As a member of the WomenEd community, I have seen first-hand the impact of this community and, more profoundly, the impact that a sense of place and space to share stories and obstacles has had on my life, on my leadership journey and on the lives of so many women within the community. The WomenEd values – abbreviated to the 8 Cs of clarity, communication, connection, community, confidence, collaboration, challenge and change – lie in the face of the crisis described in this chapter. Their growth from a founding group of seven to over 20,000 members demonstrates the need, particularly, I would argue, in this current education climate, for women leaders to be connected and supported.

BAMEed

In these times of growing disillusionment about the system and about the way in which leaders and teachers can navigate the pressures of the sector, more and more grassroots groups have sprung up to provide solutions. Another such group is BAMEed, 'a movement initiated in response to the continual call for intersectionality and diversity in the education sector'. BAMEed exists because schools still find it a challenge to recruit and retain an ethnically diverse pool of teachers. Three conferences on, and BAMEed has gone from strength to strength, offering support and expertise to those BAME colleagues wanting to make a move into teaching itself or leadership.

Education Twitter

In many ways, these grassroots movements started on Twitter and talk to a very powerful resistance to the current climate. The huge community of educators occupying social media spaces and giving voice to the variety of concerns and anxieties about working within the sector support others to find their voice.

The Twitter education space can, of course, act as an echo chamber, sending the familiar voices of the inspectorate, education policy writers, regional schools commissioners (RSCs) and local authorities around and around the halls. I have found that these voices, at times, add a layer of doubt, fear and anxiety to my work, having me believe momentarily that it is I and only I who cannot keep up with what is required of me. But what is refreshing about Twitter is that it has democratised communication, and within minutes the educator voice can be spoken and heard in the face of policy changes, Ofsted announcements and so forth. Although bewildering in its scope for much of the time, knowing that you are in the good company of others who feel the need for change in a system that feels utterly overwhelming is golden.

Nourished Collective

The nuances of context mean that grassroots groups, LeadMeets, TeachMeets and BrewEd events can meet and are meeting the needs of so many educators grappling with how to improve the sector and find ways of thriving within it. Indeed, my own network, Nourished Collective, provides a space for just these considerations and acts as a bright spot for those navigating these tricky times in schools.

*

This chapter has set out to shine a light on some of the ways in which centralised control is still very much alive in what we have come to regard as a relatively decentralised education sector. In recognising that there are still numerous controlling stakeholders beyond the school, we can see that enacting autonomous leadership in schools is harder than it might initially seem.

The personal toll on leaders and teachers of this lack of autonomy and the high-stakes environment is evident in the numbers of people leaving the profession. This means that in many ways the education sector as we have known it feels to be on the brink of dissolution. However, there is hope and there is a way forward. Grassroots organisations have sprung up to support those people who want to develop a more profound sense of self and who want to influence change in their workplaces. These organisations are working towards a new narrative of leading and teaching in the education sector. Like the chapters of this book, they believe there is another way.

Key questions to help you light the way

1. To what extent do you see your identity as distinct from the identity of the school?
2. Do you take steps to recognise the personal toll that leadership takes on you?
3. Are you alive to the challenges felt by new teachers in your organisation?
4. Do you take steps to normalise the experiences felt by staff who are struggling?
5. What is your vision for the education sector and for everyone in it? How can you light the way?

3 Schools on the threshold

Chapter overview

This chapter takes a look at how schools have become a crucible for societal pressures and internal pressures. It considers the extent to which government leadership of the sector has exacerbated these pressures as a result of ceaseless initiative drives. It considers the ways in which autonomy has been chipped away at and how accountability measures impact for us all. Why? Because to light the way we need to decide on the kind of climate we want to create in our schools of the future.

While in many ways our schools are melting pots in which cultural assimilation takes place and in which unique school cultures evolve, they are also places that need to withstand the storm of system and societal pressures. In this chapter we will look at some of the pressures that are brought into our schools on a daily basis. These pressures – funding, mental health and initiative overload as well as accountability measures – are things that school leaders need to finds ways of accommodating.

How is overwhelm manifested in school life?

When our already stressed-out teachers go into school, lots of them find a system under pressure – for many of the reasons identified in Chapters 1 and 2 of this book. There is something so breathless and so panic-ridden about the pace of life in our schools. The accepted wisdom that change is the only thing that can be relied upon does not help. But what has caused this sense of overwhelm and what is the impact on our schools?

Headteacher turnover

As we saw in Chapter 2, page 17, workforce changes are commonplace among teaching staff and something just as concerning is the turnover rates of headteachers. As the NFER points out, 'Retention rates for primary headteachers fell from 94 per cent in 2012 to 92 per cent in 2015. For secondary headteachers, retention fell from 91 per cent in 2012 to 87 per cent in 2015' (Lynch et al., 2017). I can't help wondering at the impact of such turnover rates on a system that ought to be more dependent on memory, legacy and stability because these things anchor us to our past and to something secure in uncertain times.

New initiatives

Added to the flux of the teaching workforce are the successive changes at government and policy level. We have an education system to which things are added and little is taken away. In many schools, new initiatives are dressed up as innovation and, as a profession, we seem to believe that innovation is necessary to strengthen the argument for change.

The reality for most headteachers is that they are presented with an endless buffet of new initiatives that are sold as innovations. It would take a will of steel to remain focused on your school's 'one thing' and to ignore the clamouring on Twitter and on all the other compelling channels persuading you that school improvement can be found using their particular approach. The average senior leadership team comprises leaders who hold extensive portfolios. This means that there can be a tension between wanting to drive school improvement, resisting the next shiny thing and supporting their staff in managing workload. Sometimes the temptation for the shiny thing that has, to all intents and purposes, revolutionised the school up the road proves irresistible. The knock-on effect is felt by middle leaders, who then find themselves in a position of having to manage competing priorities and initiatives.

I am a firm believer in the human being's ability to hold multiple ideas in their head at the same time, yet I doubt very much the ability of any middle leader to manage a significant teaching load, leadership of a team, the implementation of a new curriculum, a new approach to assessment, a change to pedagogical approach and the introduction of a new behaviour system. But, in some schools, because of our addiction to change, this is what we are asking of middle leaders.

Financial pressures

Financial pressures have hit schools hard and this is a significant contributory factor to the overwhelm felt by educators. When I was headteacher of a large secondary school, my feelings of overwhelm were underscored by knowing that there would not be enough money to deal effectively with almost any issue that arose.

There were mornings that I would drive to work through the rain knowing without a doubt that the art department would be submerged in water and that, other than the same temporary fix, it would be unlikely that we could do anything about it. As the winter drew in and the dark evenings arrived, there would be questions over the quality of lighting in some areas where the cost of replacing lights overrode the usage the room got. In some areas of the school, we knew the heating would fail. The rooms would be cold in winter and, as summer emerged, those same rooms would be too hot to work in and unbearable to teach in, given the lack of working blinds.

Being required to do more in schools with fewer resources is most uncomfortable, and managing the bombardment of questions I fielded as a headteacher about what could be done, what I intended to do and how things were going to improve was a significant challenge.

If it was a challenge for me, it was a nightmare for my staff. It was the teachers in classrooms who were dealing with the blinds that were broken, and it was the teachers planning lessons around the lamps that had blown in their projectors. It was the teachers who were being expected to teach to ever-increasing numbers of children and wondering quite how they would cope with it all.

Choice overload and information overwhelm

Curiously, the wisdom with which heads are appointed to do their jobs and the diligence that goes into the headship recruitment process are rarely matched by the respect they receive and the trust they are given to use that very same wisdom they demonstrated at interview. An individual headteacher can't trust they have the absolute autonomy to go their own way. The average headteacher rarely believes they are the master of their school's destiny and that they can choose to act in whatever way they think is most appropriate. Headteachers are considered brave to step out of the box and heads that do are remarked upon. It is decidedly tricky for headteachers to navigate a system awash with initiatives and new approaches and to judiciously choose which action is right for the school and the context. It is trickier still to choose no new activity.

The education sector has become a giant marketplace. Schools across the UK spend nearly £900 million annually on education technology (Manning, 2017). Thousands of companies tout products and services that they want headteachers to try out. Each product talks to the very pain point that most headteachers face – making the most of the scant resources they have available to improve or sustain outcomes rapidly.

Added to the number of products in this giant marketplace is the extraordinary volume of state-driven initiatives and policy changes that take place each year. As a headteacher, I used to be a big fan of Policy Watch, partly as I always had the nagging sense that there was something I hadn't managed to keep abreast of. Policy Watch was a blessing and a curse. Yes, I was up to date on all the policies and changes to legislation and up to date on the consultations, green papers and white papers. However, sadly, I was completely overwhelmed with how to respond to the deluge of information.

More often than not, I took on the impossible and tried to incorporate the new policies I had learned about into an ever-growing portfolio. I shared what I felt was relevant with senior leadership team (SLT) members, only to find they hadn't had time to look at them and I'd left them similarly deluged and overwhelmed as a consequence. Unsurprisingly, my time spent with Policy Watch was short-lived.

The problem with these policy updates was that this was not an area within which I could be judicious. Because of the accretion of education policy, nothing was ever taken away; no job was no longer needed. More was expected of me, and the burden felt intense.

I remember talking to my mother one evening about the river of initiatives that I felt I needed to embrace but that threatened to drown me. She suggested I didn't take them all on. It sounds like common sense. However, the stakes in schools have been identified as being so high (and for so long) that most headteachers and certainly most teachers are terrified of stepping away from what is recommended.

For headteachers, the likelihood of losing one's job should a set of results not be deemed good enough is pretty high. There are links made between the outcomes of tests at primary school or GCSE results and headteacher capability. The suggestion is that a headteacher has not done their job if results dip. The result of this overreliance on end-of-key-stage results as an indicator of success is a system in which Ofsted, local authorities and multi-academy trusts (MATs) view school performance often in isolation from other factors. Thus, for good reason, headteachers rarely feel empowered to step away from what is being mandated or recommended by these authoritative bodies.

The role of the inspectorate

Ultimately, the inspectorate has a lot of influence. Neither MATs nor local authorities are powerful enough to step away from what the inspectorate is expecting to see. No matter how inventive, imaginative or contrary an education establishment or body might want to be, the stakes are too high when the reality bites.

The dangers of an inspectorate that is the tail that wags the dog are evident. However, when it is the inspectorate that sets out the framework within which the narrative of the school must fit, they set the agenda for the education system. This can, and often does, strike a note of dissonance for school leaders and teachers who are working in schools that, try as they might, can never match the success of the school up the road, because their distinctive context makes it difficult to do so even with the same inputs.

The chipping away of autonomy

I believe that, thank goodness, there is no one way to lead a school. What makes a headteacher decide to step up and say, 'I can do this' is probably a sense of rugged individualism and perhaps a belief that they can 'light the way'. The high-stakes accountability model of school improvement chips away at this individualism and argues that the diverse and many ways in which a school could be judged as 'good' are irrelevant. This model of school improvement believes in one set of information and thinks this is the only way of measuring success. It also determines a specified and short window within which this must be achieved.

The individual who aspires to incrementally improve a school through longevity of service is cast aside in favour of a headteacher who is focused on quick outcomes. The latter brand of leadership demonstrates time and again that it can meet the high stakes head-on. As the pressure to improve schools swiftly is paramount, the former often proves that it cannot, as it is not given time to do so.

The effect of this is that an understanding of what autonomy really means is completely lost in the system. Leaders who play the game of careful examination entries and providing options for children that limit the enjoyment and diversity of their experience can make it work. Similarly, leaders who use exclusion to advantage the outcomes of a year group will find a place in this current reality. Those who tailor everything in their schools towards being 'outstanding' in Ofsted terms appear to be the autonomous, influential and successful leaders of our time but sometimes they are quite the opposite. These are the leaders for whom failure is not an option, but the cost is high. These are the leaders who, in refusing to step away from the dogma of a system overburdened with instruction, contribute to a system in which everyone is made a puppet.

There is a trickle-down effect for teachers working in a system in which accountability has such high stakes. The pressure for teachers to ensure that the children in their classes achieve ever higher grades and get ever better outcomes is enormous. While, in many schools, this can crudely be linked to teacher pay and performance management and threaten the livelihood of teachers, this is not the most damaging effect. The danger of a high-stakes system for the teacher is that it fails to tap into the expansive, exploratory and creative nature of the teacher – the artist. While it can, of course, be argued that the experienced and jaded teacher has no positive impact on student outcomes, playing to the lowest common denominator and suffocating all teachers to counterbalance this is an oversight and an overreach.

Teachers who come into a system because they believe they have something distinctive to offer soon find that what is wanted is not that distinctiveness but a very narrow set of skills and behaviours that will lead to a particular set of outcomes. Whether or not they will meet these outcomes is checked through lesson observations and book scrutinies that are often designed to counter a leader's sense of discomfort with what might not be happening. Indeed, these activities are often there to soothe the anxieties of leaders and reassure them that the exact things that they set out to achieve will be achieved and are evident in classroom practice. What many teachers find is that there is very little room for practitioner exploration or script improvisation.

The pressure on teachers to manage the shame, embarrassment and heart-in-mouth moments of exam results has them leaving the profession in numbers. But, more importantly, the compromises they need to make in the way they teach, the limited curriculum they are often asked to deliver and being required to provide an educational experience for children that sometimes lacks depth and breadth have them leaving because this is not what they envisaged when they became teachers.

The accountability measures in schools do seem to be having a significant impact on teacher workload, with many teachers experiencing the stress and effects that the unreasonable demands of meeting accountability measures are having on their lives.

High-stakes accountability: the impact on children

Our children also bear the brunt of this high-stakes approach to school improvement. They are ultimately the ones being tested. The unintended consequences of a system in which leaders squeeze teachers are that children feel both the burden of responsibility to do well for their teachers as well as the stress of being tested.

In a report commissioned by the National Union of Teachers (Hutchings, 2015) on the impact of accountability measures on children and young people in the UK, there was evidence that because teachers focused their teaching very carefully on the tests, attainment improved. The same report indicates that, despite all the pressure to the contrary, there is 'no evidence as yet that accountability measures can reduce the attainment between disadvantaged pupils and their peers'. What the report did find was that disadvantaged pupils are more likely to become disaffected by high-stakes testing and a cycle of failure.

We are witnessing in our schools a rise in mental health and anxiety-related disorders, and inevitably some correlation between the increase in high-stakes testing and these disorders can be observed. I have been struck by the number of teachers and parents who have felt encouraged to speak out about the untenable levels of stress and anxiety that testing at primary and secondary level has placed on their children or children they know. Joanne Boofty (2018), writing in the *Independent*, says that as a parent and teacher she took her child out of school to avoid the SATs, as she felt they created the antithesis of a growth mindset.

One primary headteacher I talked to was quite tearful about the impact that the Key Stage 2 SATs were having on his niece. Despite him witnessing the pressures on children within his own school, seeing the stress it caused within his own family gave him another perspective and one that made him reconsider the necessity of these tests at all.

Mental health in modern Britain

Schools are microcosms for the rest of society. This means that we experience the tumult and the delight of everything that takes place beyond the school gates. Life in modern Britain certainly has ramifications for the adults and children in our schools and this becomes evident if we look in more detail at mental health.

Findings from the Adult Psychiatric Morbidity Survey 2014 (McManus et al., 2016) show a steady and consistent rise year on year in the number of people living with severe symptoms of common mental health disorders. It probably wasn't until I took on the role of headteacher that I began noticing the steady creep of common mental health disorders that staff were experiencing in my schools. Known as depression, anxiety disorders, panic disorders, obsessive-compulsive disorders and post-traumatic stress disorder, I began to find that these illnesses were becoming more and more noticeable in my settings.

Sometimes, when talking to staff members about their lives outside of school, they would reveal that they were coping with an illness of this nature. Some colleagues would divulge that they had experienced a prior bout of depression many years ago and were worried about the school context or the school climate bringing it about again. In my schools, there were staff trying to cope with the mental health of their partners, their children or other family members. And there were also staff managing the impact of grief. I recall being quite shocked at the burden many were carrying.

More recently, I have felt that in being open to having conversations about adult mental health, more and more staff members have come forward to talk about how they are coping with the impact of common mental health disorders in their lives.

But it isn't just mental health disorders staff are coping with. For many staff members, balancing life with work is hard. The more I talk to teachers who are parents, the more I am convinced that parenting and working in a school is an almost impossible balancing act. Teacher-parents are racing every day to collect their children from nurseries and after-school clubs. For these colleagues, just one unforeseen event means the whole pack of cards topples. And then, of course, there are the teachers who are not parents but who feel that the black hole of workload threatens to gobble up all of their available time.

Schools: the melting pot

In our schools, the mental and spiritual health of our workforce meets the mental and spiritual health of children growing up in exceptional times. These are times that have seen rapid growth, particularly in communication and the ability to be permanently switched on and allegedly connected and yet paradoxically to feel so disconnected.

A study (Power, 2017) found that teenagers felt under significant pressure to make themselves available 24/7 and experienced anxiety if they did not respond to texts or posts immediately. It also found that one-fifth of secondary school pupils would wake up in the night and log on 'just to make sure they didn't miss out'. In 2019, yet another piece of longitudinal research on the impact of social media on children was announced in the *Guardian*. In the same article, the most recent official statistics on mental health in England are cited and an alarming finding is highlighted: '11- to 19-year-olds with a [mental health] disorder were more likely to use social media every day than those without' (Siddique, 2019).

Social media use is also affecting our staff. According to Ofcom (2018), Britons spend, on average, a day per week online, and the average Brit checks their phone 28 times per day. This loss of time to social media, outsider opinion, other people's lifestyles, suggestion and 'noise' inevitably takes its toll.

Whatever the role of social media, the mental health of our school communities makes the pages of educational literature daily, and the crisis in school funding underscores in the cruellest of ways that we cannot meet the growing unease of children living in the 21st century. Self-harm, anxiety, suicide and depression are all unfortunate features in our schools. When you add to this the tumult experienced by many of the adults in our schools, the melting pot of schools becomes a crucible within which explosive, heightened and raw emotions can arise. Indeed, the melting pot of schools probably has less to do with the collective gathering of people from different backgrounds and cultures and more to do with the exaggeration and distillation of the intensity of life in modern Britain.

It is hardly surprising then that our schools feel like places in which anything could happen and in which everything usually does.

Key questions to help you light the way

1. Are you aware of the mental health of your staff?
2. Are you mitigating the burden of initiative overload?
3. Are you encouraging a healthy degree of autonomy in the classroom and from your leaders?
4. Is your school mitigating the turbulence of life in modern Britain to provide stability and a safe haven for your school community?
5. What climate would you like in your school and every school? How can you light the way?

PART 2

School leaders as torchbearers

4 The job of the school leader

Chapter overview

This chapter presents an understanding of leadership and the role of the leader as an antidote to the crisis we are facing. It sets out what leadership is as well as exploring the styles of leadership that leaders can utilise. It explores the reasons we now need ethical leadership and illustrates how we can lead our staff with moral purpose. Why? Because to light the way through challenging times, we need leaders who understand leadership, understand how to be good leaders and are prepared to take on the role full-heartedly.

The first few chapters of this book have set out some of the challenges to leading in the education sector. They have explored some of the ways in which external societal pressures impact on school leadership as well as the ways in which the system itself has led to a high turnover of staff and the ways it potentially impacts negatively on the mental health of school communities.

The remaining chapters of this book set out to light the way towards ethical school leadership in which autonomy is nurtured and to share strategies leaders can use to overcome some of the challenges we are currently facing.

What is leadership?

We talk about leadership a lot in the education sector. However, there is perhaps a sleight of hand in the way that we speak about leadership and what we expect from our education leaders. I say this because, despite claims that what schools need are good leaders, what a system such as the one we have been describing so far in this book asks for would seem to be good managers.

John Kotter, Professor of Leadership at Harvard Business School and a renowned thinker on leadership and management, describes management as 'a set of processes that can keep a complicated system of people and technology running smoothly' (Kotter, 1996). Similarly, Warren Bennis, an American professor regarded as influential in the field of leadership studies, describes the manager as one who 'focuses on systems and structure', who 'has a short-range view' and who 'maintains' rather than develops (Bennis, 2003). What unites these definitions of management – and many others – is that they involve organising work or, as Vineet Nayar, a leadership and management expert in the field of human potential management, puts it, 'controlling a group or set of entities to accomplish a goal' (Nayar, 2013). Management is about having direct power over people, line-managing others and ensuring that they get things done – managers manage tasks.

In the current education climate, what could be better than a proliferation of managers? Individuals who are prepared to count the value of small units of information and who have no view or influence over the big picture. Individuals who can ensure that outcomes are reached through the management of other people and who are comfortable operating within the status quo rather than changing, reimagining or re-envisaging it. What could be better? Well, leaders could be.

Who are the leaders?

Leaders are described with a refreshing difference, and they come on the breeze of revolution and with a buzz of excitement. Nancy Duarte, American speaker, writer and communication expert, captures the importance and the essence of leadership in her book with Patti Sanchez. They describe leaders thus: 'They stand at the edge of the known world, patrolling the border between "now" and "next" […] guiding people through the unexpected and inspiring them to long for a better reality.' (Duarte and Sanchez, 2016) In this, Duarte and Sanchez capture the leader's role as one that is visionary, that sees the potential, that nurtures a means of reaching a better reality and that takes the responsibility of getting others there as part of the work. The image of the patrol person, watchful as others rest, is powerful as it highlights the vigilance and courage that are needed by leaders. Duarte and Sanchez also offer a powerful incitement to take up the role: 'Some say being a torchbearer is a burden. Some say it's a blessing. Either way, those who light the path are the ones who change the world.'

While no one I have read quite captures the searing brilliance of what leadership can be, there is some universal agreement and synergy with Duarte and Sanchez's views expressed by other noted leadership and management gurus. Returning to John Kotter, he believes that leadership is 'about aligning people to the vision, that means buy-in and communication, motivation and inspiration'. Quoted in the *Guardian* (Ratcliffe, 2013), Kotter continues that 'if the world is not changing and you are on top, then management is essential, but more leadership really is not', going on to explain that leadership is always about change.

The future-orientated nature of leadership with change at its heart is, I believe, something we should seize, especially given the difficult times we are witnessing in education. For all of those who yearn for change and better times, understanding the skills of leadership and honing the attributes of good leadership feel like critical tools.

Can anyone be a good leader?

Having established what leadership is, let's now move on to consider how to do it!

When I was first training to lead, and participating in my first 'leading from the middle' programme, there was much talk of leadership styles. There was an encouragement for us as leaders to consider the kind of leadership style towards which we leaned. In their book *Primal Leadership*, Daniel Goleman, Richard Boyatzis and Annie McKee (2013) set out six different leadership styles, which certainly dominate discussion about approaches to leadership enduringly. It is made clear by the authors, and also whenever anyone asks you what style of leader you are, that it doesn't matter. Indeed, most leaders will have attended training in which they would have been told that there is no hierarchy and that different leadership styles can be used for various purposes.

The six styles of leadership

The key point is that the different leadership styles can and will be used for different reasons, depending on the season of the school or any other specific reason. It helps to be clear on what the styles are in order that you can have awareness of what is in your toolkit and call on any one of these styles if you should need to.

The affiliative leader

This leadership style favours people and brings attention to the value of people and their emotions, more so than tasks and responsibilities. Affiliative leaders would tend towards keeping people happy and wanting to create a sense of team and team harmony. Affiliative leaders are 'people people'. They know how to motivate individuals, and they know how to build trust, through showing genuine interest in others, flexibility, allowing other voices to be heard and giving people in their team the freedom to innovate and take risks.

The authoritative leader

The authoritative leader motivates their team towards a clearly articulated vision. This leader knows where the team is going and is confident about how to get there. This leader is good at articulating every team member's role in getting to the destination. The authoritative leadership style is seen as being especially useful when an organisation has been adrift or has lost its way, as it can be implemented as part of a new vision-setting approach or when clear direction is needed.

The coaching leader

According to Daniel Goleman (2000), despite the proliferation of coaching in the workplace, and indeed in education settings, the coaching style is one of the least used leadership styles. It could be because this style is perceived to be a time-heavy approach to take with teams. Because of the focus on ongoing dialogue, the coaching style ensures that members of the team know the expectations of them. This style also allows for regular opportunities for individuals to reflect on their contribution to the team's work and/or their performance. The coaching style is perfect when members of the team value reflection and feedback and want coaching, but it is ineffective when employees don't want to change. The value of this style is that the leader need not always tell and direct, as there is so much that can come from the team members themselves.

The coercive leader

The coercive style is considered the 'command and control' approach to leadership. It is the 'do as I say' model that might only be useful in times of crisis or when an extreme organisational turnaround is needed. Most are keen to note that this style of leadership has the potential to break individuals and team members if used as the sole mechanism for leading people and change.

The democratic leader

The democratic leader is one who is keen to build consensus through everyone participating. The democratic leader wants to hear what people think and amplifies the voices of all people in the team. This style places emphasis on flexibility and this is combined with well-honed listening skills. The upshot is that motivation can often be high for those working with democratic leaders. However, the drawbacks of this approach to leadership can be that too much time is spent listening and considering and not enough time is spent having an impact and moving forward.

The pacesetting leader

This style of leadership is also one that may not be necessary to use as a dominant style or even very much and it is, again, a style suited to the situation in which a quick turnaround is required. The pacesetting leader will set far-reaching and ambitious goals and will include themselves in the achieving of these goals, often leading by example. In a sector that has been embracing a more 'radically candid' style, the pacesetting leader is a success and can tell it how it is, and team members know when they are falling behind or not meeting the mark. However, while this might be motivational at first, this style can quickly sour team relationships and dampen team spirit, as people feel confused or overwhelmed by the expectations of their leader.

*

As Daniel Goleman (2000), writing for the *Harvard Business Review*, points out, 'few leaders have all six styles in their repertory, and even fewer know when and how to use them'. The fact is that most good leaders probably don't use all or even two of these styles. However, they may have used another special source to work out what was needed and when. This Goleman describes as the 'emotional intelligence' that underlies each of the styles of leadership.

Emotional intelligence

Goleman explains emotional intelligence as 'the ability to manage ourselves and our relationships effectively'. The four capabilities of emotional intelligence are detailed on the following page, and these capabilities and their components underpin each of the six leadership styles described above. So, for example, the underlying emotional intelligence competence of the authoritative style is self-confidence, a component of self-awareness, whereas the underlying emotional intelligence competence of the democratic style is collaboration, a component of social skill.

Leadership style	Coercive	Authoritative	Affiliative	Democratic	Pacesetting	Coaching
Emotional intelligence competence	Self-control	Self-confidence	Empathy	Collaboration	Initiative	Self-awareness
Component of	Self-management	Self-awareness	Social awareness	Social skill	Self-management	Self-awareness

Self-awareness

The key skill of self-awareness is the ability to demonstrate:

- emotional self-awareness, so to be able to know and recognise one's feelings and emotions and the potential impact these have on others
- accurate self-assessment, the ability to recognise strengths and weaknesses
- self-confidence.

Self-management

The key skills of self-management include:

- demonstrating self-control, so keeping a handle on one's compulsions
- conscientiousness and the ability to follow through on commitments
- trustworthiness
- adaptability
- initiative.

Social awareness

This capability includes being able to demonstrate:

- empathy and to be able to recognise the emotions of other people
- organisational awareness, so the ability to pick up on the concerns of people at an organisational level
- service orientation or the ability to recognise what other people need and want.

Social skill

This capability includes being able to demonstrate:

- visionary leadership and the ability to influence and inspire others
- the ability to develop others
- the ability to communicate (listening well and sending out clear messages)
- the ability to be a catalyst for change, managing conflict, building bonds with people, and demonstrating teamwork and collaboration skills.

As we can see, different leadership styles will inevitably draw on different emotional intelligences. Still, if we know we are more attuned to a particular leadership style, for example coercive, rather than thinking, 'I must try to be more affiliative', we can attempt to develop the emotional intelligence that underpins the affiliative style. Thus, the work becomes to cultivate more collaboration skills and more empathy.

A crisis in leadership

As all leadership styles are useful, depending on the context, the question as to whether great leaders are born or created as a result of circumstance is an interesting one.

It is interesting because what we have witnessed in recent times seems to be a dearth of good leaders. There has been a shortage of world leaders able to demonstrate an underpinning of emotional intelligence or indeed a vision that is so tightly held that we have a sense of the leader's ambition, even if we don't agree with them. This is backed up by a 'Survey on the Global Agenda' (Shahid, 2015), in which 86 per cent of respondents believe we have a leadership crisis today. It is understandable. Whatever the colour of your politics over the last two decades, the world has been watching on as those in positions of power and occupying the highest offices have displayed poor leadership. Their actions have certainly challenged our notions of how good leadership looks.

Perhaps as an attempt to curry favour with an apathetic electorate, a populism has sprung up in politics. These political leaders insert themselves among the people through fluency with tools such as Twitter and other social media channels. However, the tools themselves and this fluency threaten to sometimes undermine the status of these political leaders and put on display their compromised compass.

What has emerged, in some cases, has been a rather unpleasant brand of politics. This is a political stance that leads with a personal attack, with a lack of measured response, with hateful words said about other nations and radio silence on issues of morality. When the top offices are filled with people who believe they are above the law, and with those who will openly admit that they can find ways around the law, one does have to wonder what leadership can come to mean for society.

If you take a look at the business world, things are not much better. Indeed, the leadership of some of the most powerful organisations and banks in the world gives examples of a similar crisis of leadership.

And when we step away from the secular world of industry and politics and return to the sacred, we find that, unfortunately, there is a similar crisis of leadership. Over recent years, it has become evident that some branches of the Church have chosen to cover up so many issues pertinent to human and child rights that, unsurprisingly, trust in the clergy has wavered.

The need for ethical school leadership

As school leaders, we find ourselves in the responsible position of being the people who straddle the secular and the sacred in a society that has become to a certain extent lawless (as evidenced by people right at the top), morally bankrupt and keen for salvation. With more and more people turning towards the helping professions for guidance, it is therefore incumbent upon us to accept the responsibilities of the role we now have in society and lead.

With this in mind, I think it is essential that we place moral leadership right at the heart of the job of a school leader. We talk a lot about moral purpose in education, but how many of us sit down and work out what morality means to us and how many of us map out our frameworks for moral and ethical action to guide us?

In 2017, spurred on by the crisis in leadership shown elsewhere and by growing pressures in the education sector, the Association of School and College Leaders (ASCL) commissioned an Ethical Leadership Commission. The commission developed a framework for ethical leadership (Ethical Leadership Commission, 2019) in recognition of the fact that school leaders are faced with a range of moral and ethical dilemmas week in and week out, and they needed to be held to a higher standard but also better supported to deal with these dilemmas.

What is remarkable is that, until this point, there had been no agreed-upon moral or ethical education for leaders. Despite the opportunities for school teachers to progress rapidly into leadership roles and despite there being encouragement for people who have been in non-teaching leadership roles to enter the profession, ethical learning and development had taken place independently and been entirely self-directed.

What the ASCL framework for ethical leadership does is provide an opportunity for leaders to identify what constitutes the moral battlegrounds upon which they are determined to fight the good fight.

This is important because what is right in one school or community may look different in another. Indeed, the framework for ethical leadership refers to such skills as 'selflessness', 'objectivity', 'accountability', 'openness', 'honesty' and 'leadership', which will all play out differently depending on the context of the school. It is for leaders to do the hard work of establishing for themselves what it means to be a morally bound ethical leader in their context and then deliver on this.

As a black girl growing up in rural England, I became aware of what it was like to not always be treated fairly. Countering injustice became a central tenet of my work. Because of this, I think I gravitated towards the helping professions. In turn, I gravitated in my work in schools to the places where I felt I could breathe life into social justice.

It's sometimes easier to understand your moral purpose when you work in schools with a considerable bias in favour of one group or when you work in challenging contexts. For me, a different kind of learning came when I accepted the nuance in my work. For example, when I came to lead a pupil referral service, I was faced daily with the injustice felt by the children who had been excluded from mainstream provision. For these children, several choices they had made, and usually a sprinkling of bad luck, meant they had lost a school place. I would often arrive at placement meetings for these children full of the righteousness of the wronged only to find that there was a more nuanced story, a less black-and-white issue to be dealt with. I would hear and learn of the challenges that these children presented within their schools and see the work that had been poured into making it work. In these moments, there was no clear and right choice but a hard decision that needed to be made, a decision that required openness, objectivity, integrity and honesty. Sometimes this would mean that those around the table would need to agree that exclusion was likely to be the best thing for the child themselves and possibly others, and sometimes the reverse. Leadership through these kinds of 'difficult conversations' could not be avoided. Indeed, ethical behaviour was born of sitting in the fire with the situation and picking carefully through the ashes to determine the next and right course of action.

Ethical leadership is not quick and it is not easy, but it feels good, and it can become a reflex way of acting and behaving. However, first, we need to choose it as *our* way and be proud to act accordingly.

This commitment to the endeavour and excitement to work in this way can overcome the challenges that will come along the way. This mode of working can be a way through making tough decisions about exclusions, behaviour and so forth and can become a means of children understanding what 'right conduct' looks like. It can also become a way of managing situations with adults and, in particular, a means of successfully leading adults.

Leading staff with moral purpose

Having touched upon the scarcity of autonomy in our sector, I would now like to consider one of the ways of adding it back in. I believe one of the most important jobs a school leader can perform is the kind of ethical leadership of staff that enables *them* to more effectively navigate and manage the moral dilemmas that arise each day.

The job of a school leader is to be an adult worthy of imitation for every member of the school community. We are on a journey with our staff, and we want to walk beside them most of the time, be excited as they scramble ahead with their breakthroughs and ambitions, but also be fearlessly walking ahead of them and showing them the way when necessary.

There is no point in choosing to stand as a school leader if you are not prepared to use your wisdom to guide your school community along the right course of action, to use your optimism to support them when the going is tough and to display your courage and faith in the face of the journey.

Sometimes this is difficult work. At times as leaders, we need to fight the urge to be liked as we do what is unpopular but right. As a leadership coach, this is one of the things that I find many new headteachers struggle with, trusting that the course of their chosen action is the right one even if that action upsets other staff members.

An excellent example of this comes when there is a child in the school who needs additional kinds of support but who staff feel gets away with too much and perhaps should not be in the school community. Many staff will have experienced the frustration and difficulty in trying to manage the behaviour of this child, but fewer will have had the bird's eye view of what life is like for this child beyond the school or will be aware of the consequences of permanent exclusion. It is the leader's job to make the right and, sometimes, unpopular decision to stand by the child.

Another example is when a staff member is popular and liked but going through a hard time and regularly showing up to work without the proper care and attention being put into their job. It is the leader's role to justly draw the line, to humanely say that enough is enough, to be firm and fair, and to demonstrate leadership in the way they assert the right and proper course of action. But it won't always go down well with the rest of the team.

Standing in front of staff and taking responsibility for your actions when unfortunate circumstances have forced your hand is one of the more difficult things a leader has to do – something I am certainly familiar with.

I have been on three leadership teams during periods of a staff restructuring. The first occasion was when I was an assistant headteacher. The second was when I was a newly appointed executive deputy headteacher, and the third was as an interim headteacher. In each of these situations, I learned about ethical action and confronted the weaknesses and limits of my courage.

As an assistant headteacher first encountering a staffing restructure, my role in the process was a benevolent one. I was not the headteacher, and I had not designed the new staffing structure, so my job was to work through consultation meetings with affected members of my team. In this role, I did not need to articulate the 'why' of the restructuring and, in honesty, I was not personally aligned with the decision-making. Looking back, I can see how this double-handedness was not ethical. There, right there, were the limits of my courage, and the ease with which I allowed the headteacher to bear the sole responsibility for this work was played back to me when it was one day my responsibility to be the headteacher leading on similar decisions.

As a newly appointed deputy headteacher, I was, again, not responsible for the new structure in design. However, I was determined to back the decisions that had been made 100 per cent. I set out, therefore, to be constructive and positive about the new way forward. There were significant financial implications to what had been the existing staffing structure, and these would ultimately threaten the long-term stability of the organisation, so the ethical impetus was to secure jobs and an adequate provision. Nevertheless, charged with delivering these messages in countless union briefings, in one-to-one meetings and to a drama hall full of angry people, my courage wobbled, my voice shook and the limits of my confidence were significantly challenged.

More recently, I was responsible for the design and the delivery of a new staffing structure, again for financial reasons. I don't agree with a system that has squeezed the education sector to the point of having to drop the axe on people's jobs. I don't think we should have to use the language of 'deleted posts'. However, I do feel that if you are in a leadership role in our current system, then the moral obligation is to act in the best interests of the children and operate within the fiscal means of the school. In this case, my role as a leader was to make sure that the process, although painful, was conducted in a way that maintained everyone's dignity. If people were angry and upset (as they were), it was my job to face that anger and upset. If people wanted to use formal means to challenge the decisions I had made, I needed them to know that I respected their choices. Refusing to hide from my staff, avoid them or silence them was the route I opted for, and it is the route I would choose again.

How to create your own code of ethics

As a school leader, you will develop your own code of ethics, which may look very similar or very different to mine. To reflect on and start creating your code of ethics, try the following steps.

1. Write down a list of the beliefs you hold about school leadership and, more importantly, the reasons why you hold these beliefs. It can be helpful to separate out the beliefs that are genuinely yours from the beliefs that you have adopted and which do not necessarily resonate with you.

2. Commit in writing to your 'why'. Why is it important to you in your leadership role to have a personal code of ethics? Try to get this explanation down to one paragraph and make this paragraph the heading for the next section.

3. Write a list detailing the ways in which your beliefs will influence your behaviours and actions as a school leader. Thus, your belief in equality might lead to the statement: 'I will treat all those I come into contact with equally and fairly.'

4. Write out a handful of challenging situations in which you would be called upon to bring this code of ethics to life. Try to examine the ways in which this personal code of ethics could help you in the situation or with decision-making.

*

This chapter has set out to explore what leadership is as well as the leadership styles that can be useful to any school leader, depending on the season of the school they are leading or for a variety of other reasons. It then went on to explore the emotional intelligence that leaders need to nurture in order to lead effectively. The chapter moved into an exploration of the need for ethical leadership in schools and finally set out a series of practical steps that school leaders can take in order to elicit their own ethical leadership framework, an essential tool for any leader wishing to light the way towards a brighter school system.

Key questions to help you light the way

1. Are you ready to take on your role as a community leader?
2. Do you know which leadership styles will help you light the way in your context?
3. Have you developed the right levels of emotional intelligence to light the way for your school?
4. Are you using ASCL's framework for ethical leadership or your own ethical framework to guide you?
5. Are you providing the modelling of what ethical leadership looks like in challenging times for your staff?
6. What is your vision for the leadership of your school and every school? How can you light the way?

5 Deepening your sense of self

Chapter overview

This is one of the most important chapters of the book. This chapter is about uncovering our deepest sense of self, knowing that we, as school leaders, are good enough and that we are in the right place at the right time. This chapter explores the various manifestations of the imposter syndrome. It explores coaching as a means of self-development and provides a range of tools to help leaders understand themselves and tap into their innate wisdom.

Why? Because to light the way through challenging times, leaders must have an internal ballast. This ballast does not come from external validation; it comes from a profound sense of self.

In the last chapter I described the ways that a commitment to leading with moral purpose and acting ethically can help in challenging circumstances. That being said, the ability to maintain the conviction that you are the right leader in the right place and at the right time for the school is tough. On many occasions I had to believe that I was good enough. It is this 'mind control' that so many of us need to enact because it is critical to success. In this chapter, I am therefore going to explore some of the many tools that can be used to support leaders in personal confidence and a deepening sense of self.

Imposter syndrome

For many people, the first steps to becoming the kind of leader they want to be are found in overcoming what is known as the imposter syndrome or the belief that we are a fraud or a fake, who is at some point going to get found out.

In her book *The Secret Thoughts of Successful Women: Why capable people suffer from the imposter syndrome and how to thrive in spite of it*, Valerie Young (2011) sets out a number of competence types that she suggests may hold some people back from realising their potential.

I recognise many of these in education leaders and in the women I coach who are successful and capable but who struggle with the self-belief that they are. As Young suggests, they hold themselves stringently to a series of rules or standards that they believe competent people should follow.

Young devised a workshop called 'What's in Your Rule Book' and several of the rules she elicited from her participants ring true for many people I have coached and have certainly been true for me. They are rules such as:

If I were really good at my job (being a parent, being a scholar, etc.)...
I would always know the right answer.
I would never get things wrong.
I would never need to ask for help.
I would get things right first time.

And so on. What emerged from Young's study of the rule book exercise was that there are five different types of imposter that show up with surprising regularity. These are as follows:

1. the perfectionist

2. the superwoman/superman

3. the natural genius

4. the soloist

5. the expert.

Let's look at each in a little more detail.

1. The perfectionist

The perfectionist sets themselves ridiculously high standards, and then, when they fail to meet them or only get 99 per cent of the way towards achieving their goals, they categorise themselves as failures.

Perfectionists feel that they must be on their A-game 100 per cent of the time. They always believe they could have done better, so find it challenging to celebrate wins. In the education system, perfectionism can play out dangerously and be a quick way towards burnout, as many educators forget that we work in an imperfect system and that our efforts can rarely make it 100 per cent right.

To overcome their need for perfectionism, this 'imposter' needs to accept that things are rarely 100 per cent perfect and that flaws are excellent too.

2. The superwoman/man

The superwoman/man is the workaholic who deep down believes they are a fake and feels that they need to cover it up by working harder and harder.

This type of 'imposter' might want to gain appreciation and validation from working rather than for the work itself. They might be the first in and the last out and may well be the person sending emails at ridiculous hours of the day and night. This might also be the person who needs to prove they can manage a household, three children and their schedules as well as their job as a headteacher, their hobbies and their friends.

Again, the education sector laps the workaholic imposter up, as they can pour hours and hours into work that will never end. In this cycle, the superwoman/man can fast find their way to burnout, and to avoid it they need to find a way to accept and validate themselves in the world as someone who has earned a role and does not need to prove their worth through working harder than others.

3. The natural genius

The natural genius expects things to be quickly grasped and efficiently executed and, if they are not immediately and effortlessly easy, then they feel the shame of failure.

This type of imposter may think that they need to get things right the first time and may well have had a history of succeeding effortlessly through school and college. This person might not feel able to ask for coaching or mentorship because they are inclined to believe they are a failure unless they have all the answers, and they might avoid things that they know they haven't yet mastered.

For many natural genius types, the thought of headship will be unbearable as they haven't yet done it and may not be able to prove their ability in it yet. If they do take it on, the initial stages of failure and doubt will be very shame-inducing and hard to bear. For the natural genius to step into a comfortable position with their leadership, they need to accept that learning and modelling lifelong learning is a massive part of the work of school leadership.

4. The soloist

The soloist is the ultimate individualist, who feels that asking for help makes them an imposter. They believe that they are the only person who can do the job and that, if they need help, this must mean they are weak, which brings about shame.

Headteachers and senior leaders who are soloists are vulnerable to isolationism and loneliness, particularly in a sector that venerates the strong, and it takes real bravery for those with this competence type to come out from the shadows and seek support. Still, it is critical to accepting themselves as the right leader in the right place at the right time.

5. The expert

The expert needs to know everything and know the answer to everything. Still, deep down, they believe they will never know enough and will be exposed as inexperienced or lacking sufficient knowledge. Much like the natural genius (page 50), this makes headship tricky for the expert and could lead to the kinds of bullish behaviours that set a poor tone for leadership, as they attempt to bulldoze their way through what they are not confident with.

Many experts feel there is never enough training they could have or enough certifications they could gain. Even the most certificated feels lacking in skills and the correct training.

For experts to move through this, they need to take stock of what they do know and put it to good use, sharing it with others. For many experts, their feeling of being an imposter can be silenced by supporting colleagues who are new to the profession or those who look up to them.

*

As a school leader, I recognise all of these five competence types and the various imposter voices that have come up in my experiences of leadership and motherhood.

I was excellent at school and assumed that things should not be difficult, and I was stunned when I realised how painful failure felt for me. It was not at all like growth, but more like death. I have at times struggled to ask for help, preferring instead to go it alone and feeling the need to prove I could do it without the support of others. I have sought endless certifications to validate my knowledge and expertise in the field and been deeply critical of my fast rise through to leadership and lack of time spent in the classroom. And I have struggled with feelings of failure as I tried to set up a school five months after having my first child.

The various voices of the imposter have been shrill but, as I've softened with myself, she has quietened down. As I have found ease and more comfort with the things I can do, with asking for support and with being human and flawed, I have seen more power in my leadership of people and my life than I could have imagined.

Coaching

One of the tools that I took advantage of too late on in my second headship was coaching. You can expect me to extoll the virtues of coaching. I am a certified women's leadership coach, and I use coaching to support women working in education. But I don't think the power of coaching to superpower your leadership should be underestimated.

What is coaching?

Coaching is a form of development that centralises the coachee's ability to solve problems for themselves. As you can no doubt imagine, given the direction I have been taking in this book, it is a form of development that I am hugely in favour of, as it cuts across the tendency I have identified in the profession towards stripping away an individual's autonomy.

Although there isn't a universally acknowledged definition of coaching, most would agree that it is a personal development process that uses a range of tools to help an individual expand towards personal development and professional growth. Eric Parsloe (1999), founder of the European Mentoring and Coaching Council, describes coaching as 'a process that enables learning and development to occur and thus performance to improve'. The International Coach Federation (2019) describes coaching as 'partnering with clients in a thought-provoking and creative process that inspires them to maximise their personal and professional potential'. Julie Starr (2011) takes a more simplistic approach, describing coaching as 'a conversation or series of conversations that one person has with another'. While acknowledging the problems of trying to define and differentiate coaching from mentoring, counselling and other helping professions, Cox et al. (2018) describe coaching as:

> '[A] human development process that involves structured, focused interaction and the use of appropriate strategies, tools and techniques to promote desirable and sustainable change for the benefit of the client and potentially for other stakeholders.'

I would describe coaching as a process that enables personal growth and development through unlocking a coachee's deep knowledge and awareness and then supporting them in structuring actions and solutions for themselves. It is a process that is valuable to partake in whether you are coach or coachee.

What are the benefits of coaching?

Coaching within an education context has been demonstrated to develop leaders' sense of mastery in their roles and also their feelings of 'self-efficacy' (Rhodes and Fletcher, 2013). This means that, after a series of coaching sessions, coachees will often demonstrate an enhanced belief in their ability to perform the tasks ahead of them, largely because they have gained a sense of their behaviours and motivations as well as the context they find themselves in.

Most coaches will make clear that their work cannot be a substitute for therapy or a means of providing support to headteachers or leaders with significant mental health concerns. That said, studies have found that 'between 25% and 50% of those seeking coaching have clinically significant levels of anxiety, stress, or depression' (Grant, 2009).

How can coaching help?

A pressing reason for headteachers and school leaders to engage in some form of coaching is that the pressures of school leadership require the ability to step back, synthesise and make proportionate the work and the decisions needed.

Coaching sessions provide a great space in which to process one's work, one's approach to work and one's feelings about one's work. It is a reflective moment that is often lacking in the hustle and bustle of school life, but the opportunity to regain perspective on school life and one's role in it can contribute hugely to school and self-improvement.

Self-awareness and confidence

In a job in which many leaders feel they need to have all the answers, having access to a tool that supports self-awareness and confidence is invaluable. In coaching, coaches try to help surface the facts as opposed to the thoughts their coachees have about the circumstances. Coachees are supported in realising their levels of competence, which can have a direct impact on their confidence.

Self-regulation

School leadership comes with a duty of care and delivery of provision for sometimes many hundreds of children. It is a role that, as we saw on page 43, straddles the secular and the spiritual, with responsibility for staff, appropriate environments and managing ever-tightening budgets. It is unarguably a tough gig in which emotions can run high, and the self-regulation needed to deliver the role can be supported through coaching.

On a cold November day with a wet lunch, following a wet break, surrounded by teachers upset about leaks in the roof and poor behaviour and with an angry parent in reception, self-regulation is, as Daniel Goleman (2000) puts it, 'a leader's secret weapon'. Coaching can be a super starting point in developing it.

Motivation

Coaching is an excellent tool for moving coachees from stuck to action. As such, it is a prime tool for increasing the motivation of stuck, apathetic, tired or disengaged school leaders.

Decision-making

For school leaders who feel they have no choices, a coaching conversation can provide an excellent framework for logical decision-making. Often, space and time to reflect on the options ahead, and the variety of answers to decisions that a coachee has at their disposal, are clouded over by a fog of indecision. Coaching is a proven antidote, enabling leaders to see through the fog and emerge with confidence, clear direction and purpose.

Emotional support, empathy and encouragement

As we have seen, although coaching is not a proxy for counselling or therapy, it can be a beneficial space in which leaders can gain support. For some coachees, just having a moment to let off steam before moving on to structure a positive and clear way forward for themselves is critical.

Although many leaders fear being perceived as weak for letting these things out, the empathetic space created in coaching is a healing space to move through to find the sanctity waiting on the other side.

Leadership development

Coaching is, for many leaders, an excellent and swift mechanism for personal and professional development. Having a space in which the requirement is the review and analysis of one's owns patterns, habits and behaviours is a rare opportunity.

It provides a lens through which leaders can learn about what works and what does not work, and grow into enacting chosen practices that allow them to be the leaders they genuinely want to be.

New ideas and perspectives

For many school leaders, there will be aspects of their work that give them the sense of being lost in the weeds. The early flurry of the new term may engender feelings of clarity; new plans are followed and sometimes in school life all goes according to plan. At other moments, things are not so bright. In institutions in which things have been done in a particular way for many years, leaders sometimes need space in which to consider and reflect on alternative perspectives and approaches.

A coaching conversation, as well as enabling these perspectives to come to the fore, can help leaders see the patterns in their thinking that could benefit from some refreshing.

Retention

As much as coaching benefits the leader, it also benefits the organisation. The impacts that have been described above all contribute to self-efficacy, courage and commitment to do school leadership well. If organisations want to keep hold of their excellent leaders, coaching is a vital tool to cement their ability and their will to work for the school in question.

Finding a coach

Finding the right coach is critical, and with a sea of coaches out there offering their support to schools and leaders, it is important to determine the coaching approach you feel would work for you. Make sure you have a clear sense of what you would like to get out of the coaching before you sign up to an expensive package or long-term programme of work.

Ensure you have rapport

Any coach worth their salt will offer you a free consultation session lasting a minimum of 15 minutes. The purpose of these sessions is to work out whether the two of you have rapport. It is as important that the coach feels they can work with you as it is that you feel you can work with the coach. This session is vital and it is critical that if you have any hesitation about proceeding with the coach, you are brave enough to explore further and ask anything that might be on your mind.

Find out how they work and what methodologies they favour

Coaches have very different styles and work in a range of areas of personal and professional development. If you are a school leader, it is likely that you will be choosing to work with a leadership coach. However, in my experience of coaching school leaders and teachers at different stages of their careers, leadership coaching has often bled into life coaching, and for some people a focus on balancing life and family with the pressures of leading in schools has been a way into really addressing leadership issues.

Don't be too hung up on whether the coach calls themselves an 'Executive Coach' or a 'Coach for Working Parents'. Instead get curious about the sorts of challenges they have helped people through and the clients they have worked with in the past.

Contracting and confidentiality

You need to feel comfortable enough in your coaching relationship to be challenged by your coach, and ideally your coaching sessions will help you break through perceived barriers. For this to work, you need to be able to be open and honest with your coach. If your manager has organised the coaching on your behalf, be clear before you get started that what is shared within your coaching sessions will remain confidential and will not be reported back to your organisation.

Be mindful that no coach can offer absolute confidentiality. If they believe there may be safeguarding concerns involving a child in your care or they feel you are at risk, they will have a duty of care to report this.

Getting the most from your sessions

For the coaching relationship to work, the coaching conversation needs to inspire and motivate you to push beyond perceived barriers. As a coachee, you should therefore be willing to hear reflected back to you the limits of your thinking or action. You should be prepared for a level of healthy discomfort, and if you don't feel the sessions are adding value or helping you toward insights or breakthroughs, you should feel able to bring this up with your coach in order that they can tweak or completely change your sessions.

Other tools to develop a sense of self

As you can probably tell, as a coach and as a former school leader who has benefitted from coaching, I am a huge fan of self-development. And aside from coaching, I recognise that many tools can support leaders to gain a more profound sense of self. In this section, I will share more of the tools I believe to be really effective when deepening a sense of self, including journaling, tuning in and constructive criticism.

Journaling for leaders

Oft overlooked but a powerful means of developing leadership skill, direction and focus, journaling supports the leader without the resources for coaching.

In their study 'Making experience count: The role of reflection in individual learning' (Di Stefano et al., 2014), a group of Harvard researchers set out to find out the effect of two different sources of learning. The first of these sources was the accumulation of new experience and the second was what they describe as 'the deliberate effort to articulate and codify experience accumulated in the past' or, in other words, journaling. What they found was that participants who journaled at the end of each day, within just a 15-minute window, witnessed an improvement in confidence. They found that they had stronger motivation and were able to choose more deliberate action concerning their work.

The reason for this is that journaling gives an unambiguous framework for reflection in which the articulation of what one has experienced during a day, a project or a prolonged period can help provide a greater degree of understanding and shed light on what could be the next course of action.

As educators, working life sometimes feels mired in 'I can't do this' and 'that won't work'. There are also the internal blocks we put in place as a precursor to the blocks that we perceive others might throw in our path. Journaling can help. It enables constructive reflection and can provide a means of recognising the habitual patterns and behaviours we slip into that may impede better leadership.

How to journal

Leadership in schools is hectic. The thought of carving out any time at all for yet another (non-urgent) task can feel impossible. However, research has shown that journaling for just 15 minutes per day or even twice a week can return excellent results and improvements in leadership. There is no perfect time to journal and, indeed, the ideal time is the time that works best for you. No particular format works best. Bullet journaling is popular right now but long form, notes, drawings or some time spent with Siri will all work too.

What can be helpful is to have a framework of questions that you always answer, and below are some ideas to help get you started:

- What did you learn today?
- What significant event stood out today?
- What three things did you do well, and what three things could you have done better?
- If this day were a book, what title would you give it?
- Why am I feeling like this?
- What is REALLY going on?

One of the keys to developing a sense of self as a leader is to leave no hiding places. I'm very fond of coaching precisely because it is such an active endeavour and, although there can be the odd silence, there is a constant sieving and sorting through thoughts, feelings and emotions that keeps the noise alive in my head at least.

Journaling is an activity with a more contemplative silence around it (unless you choose to record an audio file, of course). But that silence belies a similar degree of mind chatter, and for those of us who don't like silence, it can still provide enough of a distraction for it to be distinct from activities like meditation.

However, it is often in the silence that leaders can find real pearls of wisdom and the gems that help them know what the next or right course of action might be. It is also through these moments that many leaders can come back to a sense of who they really are and find the emotional ballast they may have been seeking elsewhere.

Tuning in, not tuning out

For many busy leaders, there is much comfort derived in the moment that they can switch off and collapse into an online world, and the lure of Facebook, Twitter and Instagram provides a blessed, mindless submersion into another world. We all know what it is like to find moments, minutes, hours even, swallowed up in scrolling news feeds in order to avoid doing our work or to avoid ourselves.

Likewise, cracking open a beer, rustling open a delicious bag of crisps or bar of chocolate, or binge-watching a series on Netflix form a set of activities that we call relaxation, as they help us tune out of the business of our minds.

However, what these activities actually do is replace one set of busy mind activities with another. Yes, they may drown out the work mind, but they also drown out the true self who is in there with an answer to your anxieties and frustrations, an inner self who can calm you or sit beside you and who helps you develop a deep sense of who you are.

The power of silence

Removing all distractions when we have downtime can prove to be a remarkable tool, if a little scary, so finding time to schedule in silence is what I am advocating. And this is because, from a physiological perspective, silence has proven to have many curative effects. Knowing that regular moments of silence could help lower blood pressure, decrease stress, regulate hormones and more is good news for most school leaders. But, even more importantly, for school leaders grappling to find crucial answers to who they are and how they should act, silence can have several physiological and emotional positive impacts, including the following.

Creative solutions

Moments of silence allow for the inner voice to provide the solution that has been just out of reach. We all know that feeling of answers being offered at the edges of a nap or in that curious interim moment between sleep or wakefulness. Silence allows ideas to crystallise and new directions to show themselves. Seemingly complex pathways can find themselves unravelling in front of you and ways are made manifest.

Presence

Silence encourages you to be in the moment and the here and now, which is, of course, the only moment in which you can make a difference. Busy leaders are often fretting about the past or future thinking – sometimes about next year's results and frequently about an Ofsted inspection that may or may not be on the way. Silence can enable the grounding moments that anchor you to now and purge the anxiety of past and future thinking, unleashing self-awareness and a tangible sense of presence.

Sense of proportion

We really are very small, and even the most powerful CEO is a tiny speck in the face of the momentousness of the universe and all that is in it! Moments of silence can bring us back to the humble nature of ourselves and, at the same time, provide the means of connecting us to all that surrounds us. We can reaffirm our place in the order of things and remember that we do not need to have all the answers because we have not been designed to.

Finding time for silence

Being more mindful with our phones is an excellent start. Many of us have the things on from the moment we wake up until the moment we fall asleep, and often they make an appearance during the night when we should be sleeping. Turn on 'Do Not Disturb' and stop those notifications from bothering you!

The commute to work can often be another moment to gain from silence. Many of us fill the silence with the news, with music, with podcasts, or perhaps even by using the mindfulness app Calm. But it is worth switching the whole lot off and giving yourself space to listen to the thoughts in your head. If you try this, the trick is to just let the thoughts enter and pass without being overridden or avoided.

If you can spare the time, a walk in nature either alone or in the silent company of another is a great way to connect with yourself. Likewise, spending some morning or evening moments in meditation or simply engaging in breathing exercises can give you the much-needed moments of peace in yourself and with yourself that will provide the breeding ground for the magic to occur.

For many of us, the stream of noise and distraction is a necessary part of escaping anxiety, but the goal of deepening your sense of self is to find tools that enable you to move through discomfort. These tools will ultimately give you the confidence to lead through difficult and seemingly impossible situations and odds. Thus, when the fear of silence threatens to derail your meditative moment, actively decide to move towards it. Immerse yourself in the discomfort of feeling your anxiety. Know that you need not avoid it, fight it or reject it but that you have the strength to simply accept it.

With practice, silence will become something that you look forward to and something that you will have confidence in for its capacity to transform anxiety into knowledge and then into wisdom.

Constructive criticism

A deepening sense of self is developed through the growing ability to ensure you give yourself no hiding places, and tools such as coaching, journaling and practising the art of silence help to support you in uncovering blind spots and blocks. Another safeguard to ensuring no hiding places and space within which to grow is through inviting and welcoming constructive criticism.

As school leaders, we don't always get the daily dose of appreciation that all human beings crave and which releases the dopamine and serotonin that keep us smiling. Indeed, sometimes it can feel that all we get as school leaders is the criticism and critique from others who are not putting their hat in the ring to do the job. However, receiving criticism, while not giving us the hormone boost we might like, is an excellent means to personal development.

Constructive criticism can be sought as a means of gaining perspective on our leadership and learning from the various insights that others have about how we are going about our job. One way to do this is to take part in a 360 review, which is a process in which you self-assess against a set of leadership or role criteria and then seek feedback from members of your team you line-manage, peers and those whom you report to.

Ensuring that you conduct a regular 360 review is a great start but seeing how far into the discomfort you can take the acquisition of constructive criticism is a brave act of development.

In my last headship, I was active in gaining feedback about what colleagues and parents thought and felt about controversial issues. I found myself in many meetings in which people were angry and disappointed or would have wanted things to be another way. Hearing their dismay and their critique of my work, while deeply uncomfortable, at times gave me a mechanism for working out whether or not decisions I had taken continued to be things I could stand by. Sometimes the process led me to clarity about decisions I had gotten wrong, and sometimes I felt buoyed. The many opportunities to assess my work through the lens of other people's views taught me that I could withstand criticism and that, although I didn't necessarily enjoy it, I didn't hate it either. Ultimately, I learned that I had the ability to withstand, grow and flourish through situations that I had previously deemed to be impossible or at least very, very difficult for me to overcome.

Making use of constructive criticism

To help you elicit constructive feedback from your colleagues and to reap the benefits when you do receive it, try the following practical steps.

Keep it simple
The idea of undertaking a 360 review might well fill you with terror but there are simpler means of getting the feedback that might help you. Simply asking colleagues within your team for feedback on a project, plan or piece of work can be a good start.

Be curious about mistakes
When you know things have gone wrong or haven't gone as you might have liked, a brave position that will give you plenty of intel is to dig into what went wrong. It could be that the parent event you organised didn't run smoothly or that a piece of staff training missed the mark. To learn about yourself, develop

your ability to withstand constructive criticism and learn for the future, dive into the mistakes and ask for feedback.

How have I helped or hindered?
If you want to know what has been bugging members of your team about the way you lead, ask them. Try having a slot at the beginning of SLT or team meetings in which you ask your direct reports what about your leadership has helped or hindered them that week. The trick to making use of these sessions is to remember they are learning opportunities, not opportunities for you to get defensive. It is also worth remembering that just because someone gives you feedback that is true for them, it doesn't mean to say it is an established truth!

*

This chapter has outlined some of the ways in which leaders can develop self-awareness in order to show up and lead well. It first considered the ways in which feeling as though one is an imposter can impact negatively on leadership. The chapter then considered methods such as coaching, journaling and learning about what others think of our leadership as a means of outlining how leaders can use these tools to develop a deeper sense of self and thus confidence in their abilities.

Key questions to help you light the way

1. Do you recognise the imposter syndrome in your experience of leadership?
2. What imposter type shows up most for you, and what could you do to calm this voice?
3. How can you use coaching to develop yourself or the leaders you work with?
4. How comfortable are you with deepening a sense of self through meditation, journaling or silence?
5. How do you invite constructive criticism to learn more about your leadership?
6. How do you see a future in which inner work is a prerequisite of good leadership? How can you light the way towards this?

6 Leading with clarity

Chapter overview

This chapter sets out how to cultivate clarity even when working in schools that are experiencing chaos or instability. It considers how to formulate and communicate a vision and how to lead people through to the achievement of the vision using a set of way markers. Why? Because to light the way in challenging times is to be able to articulate where you are going, encourage your travellers to get behind you and inspire them at each stage of the journey.

As much as we might want to distance ourselves from our internal chaos and discomfort, as we have seen, the most potent way of being able to utilise it is to move towards it. The same is true for managing organisational chaos. In this chapter, we explore how leaders can cultivate a sense of clarity within the disorder of the education system and how they can use that vision and clarity to take other members of the school community with them.

The chaos of school life

During my time as interim headteacher in South Gloucestershire, one of the standout feelings was the overwhelm of trying to manage the chaos of it all.

We have been acclimatised to chaos so successfully in the education system that I believe that some of us fail to notice its persistence and enduring presence. The school system at large has presented schools with an endlessly changing diet of initiatives, as we have already explored. Governments have influenced education policy, and thus school life, at what has, at times, felt like a breakneck speed over the last two decades. And schools that haven't been able to keep pace with some of these changes or managed to implement them in a way that has led to improvements in school performance have witnessed numerous personnel changes.

We have become quite used to accepting a school life in which no two days will ever be the same, in which long-term planning is hampered by the inability to be secure in long-term funding and in which we need to expect the unexpected.

As interim headteacher in a school that needed to make significant cuts in the realm of management allowances and the infrastructure to support students with SEND, the speed at which changes were required added to the sense of chaos. But often the confusion of school life was impacted on further by the endless stream of events that were outside of our immediate control. So, for example, one morning we arrived at school to find that squirrels had (re-)eaten their way through the roofing in the temporary accommodation in which our sixth form was housed. Student artwork had been damaged, and because of the condition of the building fabric, the rooms could not be used. On another occasion, the boiler broke down, meaning that the whole sixth form needed to be closed for the day. On yet another occasion, badgers ate through cabling underneath the buildings, leading to a complete IT failure.

On rainy mornings, I would wake to the sound of rain and know that within the next hour I would discover a wholly flooded art department, such was the inconsistency of the roof drainage and guttering. During the hot summer of 2018, while others were rejoicing in the marvellous weather, I was trying to find the money to purchase blinds so that the south-facing classrooms could be used without unbearable glare. It was a fruitless search.

The chaos of managing old buildings was ever-present, and this was underscored in that year by an unexpected graffiti attack on the school. I woke to a phone call from my deputy head and heard the news that overnight children had broken into the school and daubed the grounds in offensive language about members of staff, retired and current.

These types of incident were set against a backdrop of working with children and families who were experiencing chaos in their lives. Indeed, I recall seriously contemplating my 'why' one afternoon as I accompanied a young woman to the emergency room in the back of an ambulance on a day that had looked from the start to be a busy one but that was upended by midday.

How can we embrace chaos?

There is a threat to the role of school leader if you admit that your school is in chaos. No child, no parent, no chair of governors, CEO or local authority education lead wants to hear that a school is in chaos, but I contend that part of organising the chaos and navigating through it is admitting it is there in the first place.

Chaos can cause leaders to move through several reactions. They can find themselves unable to take action; they can find that it is more difficult (or even impossible) to decide on the next steps, which can lead to operational breakdowns that inevitably have an impact on performance goals. This, in turn, can mean that leaders lose confidence in their leadership, the result of which is that team members and staff in the organisation at large begin to doubt the efficacy of the leader.

To pre-empt this cycle and to mitigate it, there are, however, several steps that leaders can take.

Remember your why

Recalling and bringing to the fore 'the why' of the organisation is a vital means of managing through chaos and learning to accept the chaos around you. The purpose of the organisation may feel impossible when all around the signs are that this is not being manifested. However, remembering your deep commitment to this purpose is the first step in planning progress towards it. Rome wasn't built in a day, but the ambition to build a world-class city was a compelling enough reason to keep going.

Communicate the vision

It can feel difficult in a cold and draughty drama hall on a Monday evening to communicate the vision for a world-class school that provides the best education, enabling every child to meet their potential because they are taught by the most exceptional staff and have access to fantastic resources. However, the job of the leader is to make the vision technicolour and to light the way towards it.

Communicating the vision is the central mechanism for moving staff through the chaos. It is the way that you ensure that they have regular opportunities to see themselves as the people who will help realise that vision, and it is critical to restoring faith and calm in an organisation.

Stick to the plan

In the thick of the chaos and when being buffeted by unexpected storms, it can feel as though it is pointless sticking to the plan as the plan isn't working.

However, the desire to step away from the operational blueprint should be resisted at all costs.

Sure, another staff meeting about an aspect of school development might feel like it needs to be postponed or shunted as a result of pressing issues that are arising concerning student behaviour, for example. However, to keep the wheels on, school leaders must model their unwillingness to be derailed.

This does not mean that the pressing issues of student behaviour get ignored. Not at all. What it means is that recognition of pressing matters to do with behaviour is given and that an alternative time is created to handle them. The focus then returns to the pre-published agenda, and the planned-for meeting or event goes ahead as scheduled.

Celebrate small wins

It can feel like lip service to celebrate the small things when all around bigger things look to be going badly, but this act can be profound when done well and done regularly.

Schools are made up of people who want to do the right thing and want to do things well. Sometimes chaos can mean that the daily good that people are engaged in is overlooked, and this can lead to disillusionment and the feeling that all action is pointless. Whatever the climate of the school, take time to notice what is going well and sprinkle the news of this on your team whenever you get the chance.

Listen and take care

When surrounded by chaos, leaders tend to avoid being reminded of it. This aversion to hearing any more bad news can mean that some school leaders use other people to head up whole-school meetings. It can mean that for some school leaders, they start to feel less and less at ease being out and about in the school. I mean, let's face it, we've all heard of the headteacher who locks himself in his office with a greater degree of frequency the trickier things get.

I have seen that one of the most effective ways of signalling leadership, which in turn indicates calm, is to get out among it and listen to people. What might feel like yet more staff members lining up with yet more problems or issues that require your action is rarely that. Indeed, more often than not the problems are known to you, you have been working on a plan to manage these issues and what staff want is to have your ear on them and have personal reassurance that they have been heard.

Taking care of your team by allowing them the space to vent and really listening to them enables them to get back on side with you and ensures that, for the most part, they will do their utmost to be part of the team changing things for the better.

Cultivating clarity

Cultivating clarity is a huge part of lighting the way for others, and learning how to cultivate clarity is essential. The school vision articulates the future that the school community wants for the school and, because of this, it underpins the school strategy.

How to set out your vision

The National College developed a series of materials for schools that were thinking about becoming academies and they helpfully outlined some activities to support schools in creating a new vision. They set out that schools that are successful at creating their vision start by 'thinking through the implications of the vision in practice' (National College for Teaching and Leadership). These schools will then attempt to gain a clear sense of how things will be different for all members of the school community if the vision is realised. In other words, they begin to light a path between what is now and what will be. To do this, successful schools use all lenses of the school community and consider leadership, curriculum, SEND, and teaching and learning.

In answering the following questions from the National College, schools can begin to crystallise their vision and can use their clusters of responses as a prompt to writing a vision statement:

'1. Why are we embarking on this change?

2. What difference will this change make to:

- outcomes for learners? Why?
- the attitudes of learners? Why?
- the aspirations of learners? Why?
- the relationship with parents? Why?
- the place of the school in the community? Why?

3.   How have others approached establishing a new vision for the future of their schools?'

Although writing about the business sector in their book *Illuminate*, Nancy Duarte and Patti Sanchez's (2016) approach to creating a vision chimes with the above. They argue that if the vision is to be realised, the vision must be held and shared by all members of the team: 'They are the ones who can make your dream a reality, but only if it becomes their dream too'.

As a leader, to ensure that you take people with you, the authors of *Illuminate* agree that you must first listen empathetically to your team to ensure that you have seen the journey through their eyes. They believe it is essential that you are clear on how your team will be affected by the journey so that you can craft communications with them that resonate. When leaders really listen to their teams, they create an empathetic awareness of the others who will be following along the path of the journey, and the call to action when it comes (the call to leap = to fight or climb) is more likely to be met with a resounding 'Yes'.

I read *Illuminate* as soon as it came out in the year that the school I had set up and where I was founding principal was about to move into new accommodation. The school was expanding for the third year in a row and had needed to withstand many storms. We knew that Ofsted would be in attendance at some point in the school year, and I was keen to find a way through the chaos of being a start-up school – a school with an alternative curriculum, an alternative teacher training route and a parent body that was conscious, critical and outspoken – and the accountability system of the state sector looming.

The premise of *Illuminate* is that it is the leaders who are the people who not only anticipate the future but who 'shape the future and bring it forth'. In the book, the authors argue that, in order to be healthy, organisations need to be in constant motion and able to embrace change. For this, they need to practise well-executed and planned growth, and so the natural state of affairs in schools, with perpetual change, could be seen as an excellent starting place to begin the process of planning change.

The authors make a case for the evolution of organisations towards a desired future, which takes the form of the 'S-curve', and they plot the various stages of moving people through change towards maturation along that curve.

The book is an attempt to define the various tools that leaders need to utilise as they move their teams through the stages of the S-curve, and the toolkit the authors advocate for provides three essential tools: stories, speeches and ceremonies, and the use of key symbols. The book helps leaders create a framework for the types of stories, speeches and ceremonies that are needed at each stage of the S-curve. It does this by identifying the kinds of emotions and psychology present at each stage of the way. In separating the journey out into the 'Dream', 'Leap', 'Fight', 'Climb' and 'Arrive' stages, it becomes clear that the kinds of stories you might share in the 'Dream' stage are different to the types of speeches you might give in the 'Fight' stage.

As a leader who has navigated a fair degree of turbulence, recognising the stages of the journey I needed to go through and having a toolkit to navigate these stages lent my leadership clarity. It also lent me confidence and, dare I say, even a little excitement as we approached adversity. Knowing and being able to illuminate ahead of time that we would reach a 'Fight/Climb' stage meant that when we arrived at that stage, I knew what to say and the team knew where we were in the journey.

Dream

The dream of opening a Steiner free school was granted in 2013 after a group of committed and ambitious parents who saw the benefits of Steiner education in their own lives acted on the idea that it could be an education open to the many, not just a few. Following an extensive period of listening to stakeholders and the community, this moment of inspiration became a reality when approval was given by the Department for Education for the school to go ahead.

Leap

In September 2014, a group of brand-new children and their families were welcomed through the gates of Steiner Academy Bristol by me, their new headteacher, and a brand-new staffing body. It was a sunny September morning, and we handed out sunflowers to each of the children as we ushered them through the gates.

This act acknowledged the leap they were taking with us and marked the gratitude we all felt for the families joining us on the journey to an as-yet-unrealised future. In recognition of the fact that we did not know how this new school would find its feet, I remember making explicit reference to a new type of education setting. Indeed, my opening speech marked out a difference from where we were in the education sector and where we wanted our future to be. This is what Duarte and Sanchez call drawing attention to the 'new bliss'.

Fight

The school had chosen a growth model, unlike many new schools. And in our first year as an all-through school, we welcomed children in the Reception phase, Year 2 and Year 7.

However, in our second year, the school more than doubled, and we welcomed two classes of children into Reception, another Year 2 class, another Year 7 class and a Year 4 class. This expansion was epic and the fallout profound. Bravery was required at every moment of that year as the school tried to accommodate children with a variety of backgrounds and staff tried to accommodate children with a wide variety of needs. Meanwhile, leadership battled with the slow pace of the building works and families had their commitment to the vision of this new school tested.

Climb

The end of the school year culminated in a series of listening events during which the school attempted to reforge the commitment to the journey through shared re-visioning. All stakeholders were invited to participate and were encouraged to look back across the landscape we had traversed as well as commit themselves to the next stage of the climb.

As our third school year began and we had yet another influx of children in different years, we also opened out into our new accommodation. By this point, I had read *Illuminate* and was delighted to find the stages of our journey depicted on the page. Thus, what I set out to do was remind my team at the beginning of the year of the stages of our hero's journey and let them know that this fight/climb stage was a stage that we might be in for a while until we reached our destination.

How to communicate the vision and the route map: symbols

Duarte and Sanchez offer the use of symbols, speeches, ceremonies and artefacts as effective ways of anchoring the stage of the journey you are at with your team. Thus, our third year at Steiner Academy Bristol opened with symbology, speeches, ceremonies, stories and artefacts framed around motivating and inspiring my team through the fight/climb stage. I pictured the team as a murmuration of starlings. Indeed, the starling was the symbol that was used for the year ahead. The start-of-term speech featured facts and stories about starlings and about how they work together to form a cohesive unit. We talked about starling predators and how they act in response to these predators. I linked the symbology of the predator to the aspects of school life that could threaten our existence. Ofsted featured, as did the school budget. Mary Oliver's poem stirred the emotions. Even though we knew we would have a tough year ahead, her words from 'Starlings in Winter' acted as a call to action.

I started a staff newsletter called 'The Starling: Murmurations from the Principal' and this drip-fed short reminders of the symbol of our year together and gave visual reminders that guided the way ahead.

The impact on the staff of symbols, well-crafted speeches and the use of stories to motivate really marked a turning point in my leadership. These had always felt like tools that were in a toolkit but a toolkit that had not been endorsed in any training I had ever undertaken. It was a shift in my learning about how people can be led to do great work. I also began to realise the amount of craft that can and must go into knowing, understanding and having faith in the way ahead. It was a test to my artistic, creative and spiritual side to bring these elements into the world of school leadership, but this 'new way' made all the difference.

The year became a tough year very early on. The unusual nature of our new accommodation was testing, as was the introduction of another four classes of children. However, the staff had connected with the symbology of themselves as a murmuration of starlings. They engaged in the fight/climb stage together and, even on the most difficult of days, I would receive messages from staff with some reference to the starling.

The cards people bought each other for birthdays often included starlings. Team members would share videos of murmurations online when they felt others needed moral support. To this day, the resonance of the symbol of the starling is felt when ex-colleagues, now engaged in other projects and lines of work, share images of murmurations with me or snippets of writing about the bird. Usually, this is just because they have suddenly had cause to remember what an important chapter that period marked.

Over-communication

What sounds as though it might have been overkill in terms of the references made to the symbols of our journey, in fact fell way short of how I would now work. Indeed, what is key to the realisation of the vision and ensuring that all staff members remain with you every step of the journey is to over-communicate.

I highly recommend planning out how you will use visual, verbal and written communication to communicate your message ahead of time. This cultivation of clarity will pay dividends and mean that your message resonates with vision and reassures your team that you are exceptionally clear on the route ahead. The following sections examine how your visual, verbal and written communications might look in practice.

Stunning visual communications

Yes, we work in schools, but no, there really is no reason for this to mean that some of our most important messages (such as vision, ethos, mission and purpose) become obscured by poor presentation and shoddy PowerPoints. If the message matters, then that care must translate to the visual medium. I believe that leaders must ensure that there is a synergy between all aspects of visual presentation to keep everyone on track, to signal that there is no deviation from the plan and to demonstrate your care and attention as their leader.

In the year I have just described, I used only two or three images to communicate all messages. I created a house style and essentially indoctrinated staff into knowing that messages were vision- and journey-related when that house style occurred.

More recently, I have become fascinated by how powerfully people remember presentations and pieces of training by virtue of the images I have chosen. Indeed, my choice of images has become one of the more remarked-upon aspects of my work!

Partly it is because people appreciate at a profound level that when care and attention go into the look of something, the issue at hand must matter too. Another reason is that once you can curate a house style and set of images that accompany your message, other team members are automatically given a navigation tool, and this puts them at ease.

Having vision statements evident for all of the community to see in key areas of the school is highly important. What is also important is making sure that each stage of the journey is one that all staff hear. This helps to alleviate tension and stress and to build excitement and bravery to reach the summit.

Verbal communications

Regular meetings are vital to keeping all members of the team focused on the right thing. My leadership style is very affiliative (see page 37), so it is essential to my leadership that the team feel that I know and understand what they are facing and that they understand that I am facing it alongside them.

To this end, in the start-up school, I made use of, and would recommend other leaders make use of, clearly defined slots in meetings to engage in questions and complaints, laughter and shared wins. I cannot say enough how important it is for team members to witness you 'taking the flack'. Staff get on your side by being able to trust that you can bear the weight of being criticised or being wrong and hearing you re-state your belief that the chosen approach is the right one.

Verbal reminders of where you are headed and why the stage of the journey feels the way it does help in one-to-one meetings with staff. In my experience, I have found that it helps to check in with people and ensure that they have the strength to continue working at pace. For some staff members working at a furious pace, frustrations can occur when they receive setbacks. These staff might find that the children are not making as much progress as they would like, perhaps relationships with parents are testing them or maybe they have become unexpectedly unwell.

In these cases, drawing them back to the 'long game', reiterating the overarching vision and setting out again the stage of the journey you are on works as a mechanism to help them refocus their priorities and restore a sense of calm.

Likewise, staff who feel overwhelmed by the pace of change, challenge or discomfort during a 'leap' stage can be helpfully reminded in the course of a one-to-one meeting of the overarching vision and of the fact that discomfort and overwhelm are some of the critical feelings to experience during this stage. In other words, they are right on track.

Written communications

As we've seen, cultivating clarity is the stage that leaders go through before they attempt communication. And within each communication type, clarity is vital. The written word works across many mediums of school life – some are taken more seriously than others, and some are consumed more deeply than others.

What I have learned is that most staff place a high value on written communications and, while they hate to be submerged under a sea of emails, they appreciate the time that goes into writing a well-crafted staff newsletter or bulletin.

For the leader to ensure that these communications work, they must plan them well, craft them well and deliver them at the right moment. The key to written communications that will commit staff to the vision and revitalise them for the journey is that you view them through the eyes of the receiver. What do they need to hear and when do they need to hear it? Silence is never an option but making sure your message is well planned and executed is vital.

*

This chapter has explored the numerous ways that leaders can navigate chaos and cultivate clarity. It has looked at the stages of a journey towards school improvement, mapping a real-life school improvement journey. It then considered some of the types of communication that leaders can usefully utilise, explaining when they can be called upon.

Key questions to help you light the way

1. How confident are you at navigating turbulence and naming chaos?
2. Does your vision recognise an ambitious departure from the now to reach a golden future?
3. How well do you communicate the stage of the journey your school is at?
4. How compelling is that journey for your followers?
5. How successful are your communications about vision?
6. How can we inspire all leaders to embrace the opportunities of setting out a compelling vision? How can you light the way towards this?

PART 3

Leading staff with integrity

7 Developing staff

Chapter overview

This chapter sets out how to improve the performance and resilience of individuals and teams. It is about how to deeply engage with individuals you manage in order to overcome obstacles. It sets out a blueprint for difficult conversations that will cultivate compassion and respect. It suggests professional development that leaders can access for their staff, even on a budget. Why? Because to light the way in challenging times we need leaders who are prepared to use courage and integrity to guide and support their teams.

As I have said elsewhere in this book, one of the threats to leadership in education is the extent to which professionals' autonomy has been stripped away. This is one of the reasons why I believe that staff development must be about more than attending external training courses and internal school CPD. Rather, it must focus on improving the resilience of individuals and set out to nurture autonomy. There are a number of ways that this can be done in our day-to-day work and, although these suggestions may not seem on the face of things to be about developing staff, I believe that in the right hands they can form the basis of personal growth and confidence.

Building resilience

As a fan of personal development and as a leader always looking to improve my skills, I am an advocate for the 'difficult' conversation. This doesn't mean that I stalk the school for opportunities to haul people into the head's office or that I seek confrontation where there is none. Instead, it means that I see the value of engaging with people when that engagement may be hard. I know the importance of sitting in the fire with people through the discomfort because I know we will both come out of it forged slightly differently.

'Sitting in the fire' is a term coined by the psychologist Arnold Mindell. In his book *Sitting in the Fire* (Mindell, 1995), he charts a course through emotionally charged situations in a way that diffuses the charge for everyone and ensures nothing is repressed. Mindell believes that conflict can be dealt with constructively in a way that heals people and he believes that if we don't allow for it, we create situations in which people are forced to take the wrong kind of action.

As leaders, we must, therefore, find ease with dealing with conflict and dealing with difficult situations. This is because it is our job to hold the container for conflict and to be the ones who have utter confidence in our ability to usher others through the instability of conflict.

It is very easy in schools to succumb to descriptions of the passive nature of students and sometimes staff. We hear talk of people's failures of initiative but unless, as leaders, we are active in trying to develop people, and unless we encourage their autonomy, we are not in a position to complain.

Initiating and holding difficult conversations means that leaders create spaces of integrity that allow others to take responsibility for their actions, even when things haven't gone well. These conversations support openness, honesty and respect when handled well.

How to have difficult conversations

Over the next few sections of this chapter, I set out some advice for leaders and teachers who want to get better at having difficult conversations.

Watch your mouth

I think the term 'difficult conversations' is one of the most unhelpful terms and actually goes a long way to ensuring that these types of conversations don't go well. The amount of resistance most people have towards things that are difficult or uncomfortable is enormous, and many people would sooner run a mile than deal with what they imagine will be a situation of conflict.

Unfortunately, the school workplace can often be a place in which sentiments are disingenuous. There are some school cultures in which challenge is open and brutal and some in which care and wellbeing have become proxies for lack of challenge and fear of upsetting people. In the latter, it can be challenging to have conversations during which people might feel threatened or turned up on because the culture has not as yet supported a level of open and honest communication.

When you need to talk to someone about their performance because it doesn't meet the expectation you have of them, or the quality of work expected from all members of the team, one can expect uncomfortable feelings to arise. No one wants to upset another person, and people rarely want to be seen to be critical, so venturing into that realm can feel quite terrifying. However, as leaders, we need to bring a degree of objectivity and neutrality to the situation and take care that we are not loading what is, in essence, a conversation between two people with our anxieties about how hurtful it could be perceived to be. When we do this, we can hear and separate the emotion that may or may not come from the other person from the facts of the issue.

Be mindful and present and listen

The tools that we talked about in Chapter 5, page 56, that help leaders develop a more profound sense of themselves also enable leaders to settle into presence and mindfulness in the face of challenging responses from colleagues. If you know you need to have what could be a difficult conversation, finding space for a moment of silence and regaining a sense of presence is a really helpful place to begin.

I have a practice that helps me gather myself when tempers are fraying or when people are hostile, angry or abusive, and it goes like this. I sit upright with an open stance as if to invite the full spectrum of human emotion coming from the other person. My posture also helps me remember that I am strong enough to withstand any verbal blows. I always keep both feet flat on the ground. Feeling the stability of the earth beneath me reminds me that I am connected to something bigger than me and that I am supported. I breathe deeply and steadily, maximising the oxygen flow and calming my nerves. I allow myself to feel the heat of anger, shame, sorrow and frustration as it flows through my body and I try to recognise the feelings as vibrations that are passing through me – rather than dismiss them, recoil from them or avoid them. I use my own silence as a space to do all of the above and to allow time for the other person to feel whatever it is they are feeling and to reach the end of their tether!

Be compassionate

One of the hardest things about conversations like this is dealing with the intimacy they force. Work colleagues are rarely intimate acquaintances but conversations about performance, about failure and about personal or health issues impacting on work force a sudden and unexpected level of intimacy. This means that they are uncomfortable because the two of you are connected more forcefully than you might be used to.

The awkwardness of that intimacy for some people should be acknowledged and used as a fuel for compassion. Genuine compassion allows the other person to feel that, although it may seem that terrible truths are being revealed, they are being held in a container of care and compassion by you, their leader. Demonstrating compassion must always be a feature of this type of conversation. It underlines your humanity and commits you to respect the dignity of another human being.

Ask for and acknowledge their perspective

You must state the concern you have clearly and leave no room for doubt or confusion about what the issue at hand is. You should then ask the person you are speaking with for their thoughts or feedback on the subject.

When you ask someone to talk, you should focus your attention on really listening. Listen without interruption; put yourself in their shoes as they speak and try to understand where they are coming from. It's very important that you don't use this time to start building up all of your opposing points. This isn't the moment for point-scoring, eye-rolling or eyebrow raises. As the other person tells you their world view, listen, observe and absorb.

As people begin to reveal how they see things, they can often get tearful. It can break the tension to reach for tissues, offer them some water or suggest they take a moment to pause if they are getting upset.

Express your truth

Before you launch into what is true for you about the situation, make sure you have put in a pause. I will often take a moment to thank the person for sharing so openly with me. This is a moment to offer them another glass of water and take something to drink for yourself. These small actions will give you time to consider your response.

You must reflect on whether anything that has been said significantly changes the reason for having the conversation in the first place. It is usually the case that the emotions expressed will have made you feel like things have changed but, unless you have learned something new, allowing a performance issue to continue unchallenged is never an option.

This is the tricky bit for lots of people. It can be useful when you feel swayed by the intimacy or emotional charge of a situation to thank the person for their honesty and tell them that you feel very moved. It is good to let them know that you have a lot of empathy for the situation and that you can understand their perspective. However, you must, for their sake, be very clear that the objective of the conversation is to discuss the concern and then work out what can be done to support this person or improve the situation.

Leaders often want to muddy the waters by letting things go at this point, but for the conversation to have been worth both parties investing in, they must resist that urge.

Summarise and next steps

It is beneficial towards the end of a conversation like this to summarise the meeting. Both parties need to leave the meeting with an agreement of what took place and be clear about what happens next.

I have found that, with the benefit of understanding the person's context, it can be helpful to schedule a separate meeting to clarify the exact next steps, but the following is a useful way to end a meeting:

- Re-state the reason for the meeting.
- Summarise the other person's perspective and compassionately summarise what they said.
- Summarise your responses.
- Outline the likely next steps (for example, 'The priority is now ensuring you get the support you need. I want to flesh out the detail of this and then we can meet and discuss it further in a couple of days.')
- Book in the next meeting.

Reflect

When the meeting has ended, it can be tempting to breathe a sigh of relief that it is all over, pat yourself on the back for facing your fears and try to move on. My advice: don't. It's essential to take time to reflect.

I highly recommend creating a template based on the steps outlined above and using it as a framework for the meeting. Once the meeting is over, you can use the structure to reflect upon how well (or not) each stage of the meeting went. As you reflect, aspects of the meeting will bubble up, and these will provide an excellent insight for you as you approach your next conversation of this nature.

How to develop staff using coaching

We explored what coaching is and how it might be useful in your own development as a leader in Chapter 5, page 52. In this next section, we are going to look at how coaching can be used in schools to develop team members and support their professional growth.

Coaching is a fantastic tool that is particularly effectively when schools are going through periods of trouble. Typically, when you are managing change, unless the correct level of reassurance, communication and structure is present every day, there will be some staff members or groups of staff who feel very destabilised. Self-confidence and confidence in the organisation can be dented and people have questions and concerns that they suddenly feel ill-equipped to answer themselves. When this happens, it can feel like all roads lead back to the SLT or the headteacher.

As school leaders, we can always expect to be the people required to come up with a lot of the answers. However, I think most school leaders have felt that there are days when they are the only person who can seemingly answer any question, they are the only people able to deal with X or Y situation on the playground or in a classroom, and so on.

This can become an unhealthy cycle and, as staff members begin to recognise that SLT can't do everything, they simultaneously start to wonder why there are not more members of SLT. Before long, staff members habitually doubt their abilities to find solutions and position themselves as waiting for answers. As coaching is all about solutions, and it fuels autonomy in finding these solutions, it can be a perfect tool to structure into the daily or weekly habits of a school in order to develop staff and simultaneously alleviate pressure on yourself and SLT.

Coaching can help teachers with finding solutions to pretty much anything. Indeed, a coaching conversation can be used to explore:

- improving the quality of teaching
- managing the overwhelm of planning, marking and teaching
- work–life balance
- managing staff or team members

- dealing with challenging behaviour
- dealing with difficult parents.

Coaching skills

Coaches must know and understand the key skills of coaching before they embark on coaching others. I would always recommend that coaches experience ongoing coaching so that they continue to develop their skills and ability to empathise with the role of the coachee.

Many managers think they are coaching their team, but often they are just telling them what to do. This is not coaching and, in fact, it is often micromanaging dressed up as something else. Coaching is about helping others learn rather than teaching them. It requires patience, diligence and focus.

The following skills are needed in order to coach people.

1. Listening

Listening in coaching is active. It involves making use of non-verbal communication – keeping eye contact, and mirroring and matching postures and gestures to build rapport. Listening consists of finding comfort with silence, allowing space for both the coach and coachee to reflect and absorb what has been spoken.

2. Goal setting

As coaching is focused on solutions, coaches must be able to support the coachee in drawing out their goals. In school settings, it can often be helpful to reframe problems as goals. Thus, 'The Year 10 class are completely disrespectful towards me' can become 'I would like to develop a positive relationship with my Year 10 class.'

3. Questioning

Questioning is a vital skill that coaches need to develop. It should be used sensitively when the time feels right to find out more or get deeper, but the art of questioning also relies on coaches knowing when not to ask anything. Questions about circumstances or facts can help in the initial stages of a coaching conversation. It can then be helpful to consider what feelings or emotions are present for a coachee and what values they are bringing to the situation that colour it a particular way.

Developing staff

4. Summarising

Summarising is a beneficial tool as it keeps the coaching session on track. Summarising can provide a useful pause, and elicit whether the focus of the coaching conversation needs to shift.

5. Empathising

Empathising is the heart of coaching. Good coaches can form secure connections with their coachees because they have unconditional positive regard for the person they are working with.

How to organise coaching in schools

The logistics of organising coaching for all staff across a school are a challenge. I have worked in schools in which the commitment to embedding a coaching culture was such that a certain number of meetings in the meeting cycle were given over to working in coaching triads. I have also worked in schools in which smaller numbers of staff volunteered to be coached by staff who were trained in coaching skills.

The ambition to embed a culture of coaching can only be thwarted by a failure to commit to it. Thus, only offering opportunities for occasional coaching triads can be undermining to both the school's current focus and to the coaching itself.

That said, with careful planning, leaders might decide ahead of time on particular moments in the school calendar when a staff meeting could be helpfully given over to some staff coaching. Let's say, for example, you have a planned meeting about behaviour, safety and wellbeing. It might be a whole-staff meeting in which you would anticipate some questions or concerns to be raised by staff. A meeting like this could be opened up with a 15-minute paired coaching opportunity on behaviour.

A simple way to get coaching off the ground is to provide staff with a template like the GROW model (goal – reality – options – way forward). The framework of the GROW model means that people who are new to coaching know where they are in the coaching conversation and they have a selection of question starters if they feel stuck. As long as you make sure you give clear time reminders and nudge coaches to make sure they can get through the GROW framework within the time allotted, you can easily ensure a productive session in which staff can get stuck into an issue and generate solutions. They then begin the meeting with a problem-solving mindset and will likely generate more solutions as the session unfolds.

Headteachers and senior leaders can use coaching to model to other staff members the value placed on autonomy and solution-finding. In my last headship, I offered coaching conversations in addition to line management. These types of meeting took place at different times and so time needed to be allotted to the different types of session, but the level of frequency was such that this was an entirely manageable way of supporting my team. My SLT knew what their priorities were and often a coaching conversation gave them the space to consider what their actions would look like if they were to model best practice.

How to invest in people when you have no money

Having worked in a school in which the budget was on an almost permanent freeze, I became used to having to say no to people's requests for professional development. We would, of course, be able to squeeze the money from somewhere for cheap subject-related courses but, on the whole, we could not stretch to the kind of development I had been fortunate enough to receive when I had been a recently qualified teacher (RQT) and beyond.

In my role as deputy CEO of a MAT, the local authority was the beneficiary of support through the Strategic School Improvement Fund, which enabled us to send several people on the National Professional Qualification for Middle Leadership (NPQML) and the National Professional Qualification for Senior Leadership (NPQSL). As I was also delivering on both of these programmes, I was able to see, first-hand, the benefits for staff from across our MAT engaging in professional learning. The absence of funds to support a great deal of professional development in recent years meant that they were super keen and went all-in on their projects. They developed some excellent school improvement projects, and it was so great to watch them flourish in the role of the learner.

This experience got me thinking about the relationship between job satisfaction and personal and professional development. For, although this particular programme was being funded, I am quite sure that had I offered a number of the participants the chance to undertake a similar school improvement project in school and given them time, recognition and the platform to talk about their research, they would have been extremely keen.

I think the performance management conversation is often a missed opportunity to explore precisely what staff might choose to do in school as professional learning. Too often these conversations can end up focused on school-wide targets and exam-year-group targets. The absence of discussion about the ideas that team members have about how they would like to engage in professional learning limits their buy-in and, again, contributes to the cumulative chipping away at autonomy. Of course, given the budgetary pressures most schools are under, it may be challenging to fund external courses, so here are some ideas for professional development that can happen in school at little extra cost.

Work shadowing

If you know someone is keen for progression to the next level, use the network in your MAT or local authority to find someone for them to shadow. For this to work, it is helpful to set up a regular, recurring opportunity for work shadowing to take place. The professional learning happens when you get to see the warts-and-all version of school life and this is not always evident in a one-off school visit. If a commitment can be made across a period of time and the work shadowing is supported by a chance to reflect on a particular project or piece of work, it will be a fantastic experience and opportunity.

Now, it might feel like a bit of a pain to have someone booked in to shadow you at scheduled points over a few terms but, believe me, being shadowed really helps you focus on executing plans and upping your game. Work shadowing is a win–win – it's good to shadow and to be shadowed.

Mentoring

For some members of staff, the chance to become more skilled at mentoring would be genuinely interesting. If you can find a way to recognise this through time or other means – all the better. However, some people would be happy to be acknowledged for doing the work and be glad to become better at mentoring. For other staff members, knowing they could access a mentor would be motivating and very reassuring.

A good way to set up a mentoring programme in school is to ask for volunteers who (if you can afford it) might like to gain a qualification in mentoring. These might be keen recently qualified teachers who are not quite ready for promotion but who want to do a little more in the school.

If there is no money available to support a qualification, asking the school-based professional tutor for trainee teachers to step up and lead a session with budding mentors could be one way to set them on the right course. There are numerous books and online resources to support mentors and these could be used in the absence of someone who could deliver training.

Much like with coaching, mentors and mentees must be able to work honestly and comfortably together. If you decide to offer mentoring in school, you should be careful to ensure that there is an element of choice and that the pairings that it enables have the potential to ensure growth learning and the imparting of expertise.

360 feedback and coaching

You might not be able to afford leadership coaches or professional coaches for all your staff, but you may be able to provide a 360-review tool that supports your team in finding out, a little more objectively, about their strengths and areas for development. The opportunity to find out what direct reports, peers and line managers think of your work is a great way to get a coherent and well-rounded (well, 360) picture of personal performance. There are a number of companies that offer these and some offer ready-made review tools specifically aimed at the education sector.

If you can provide all middle leaders with a tool like this and provide them each with a session of peer coaching on their 360, it could go a long way towards helping them develop.

Improving autonomy as professional development

Schools house so much collective wisdom. Often the solutions to the problems that are facing schools can be found by putting those problems to the broader school audience and seeing what they can find as a means of solving them.

Now, I am not talking about putting everything that arises in school to the public vote. Nor am I suggesting that all aspects of school life are to be negotiated; neither staff members nor leaders have time for that. Rather, I am talking about ways of solving intractable problems that could do with a fresh approach.

Staff surveys and questionnaires and 'staff voice' activities certainly give you information about the way staff feel concerning particular issues. However, the gold is in staff expertise, which can be harnessed through them being meaningfully involved in trying to solve problems that leaders have drawn a blank on. This means feeling comfortable enough to relinquish power over particular problems. It could also mean being able to follow through on solutions that may not be your preferred way forward.

Following the implementation of a new behaviour policy in my last school, I was amazed at how we transformed negative niggles about what was not working with the new system into collective problem-solving about pinch points.

Often, making the problem bigger and not smaller helps to tap into people's collective wisdom. This sounds counterintuitive. What teacher wants to know how insolvable the problem really is? However, as adult humans, we are used to navigating the nuances and complexities of our own lives with much skill. The dumbing down of discussions in schools and institutions only serves to infantilise the adults and undercut their autonomy.

Enlarging issues like the impossibility of supporting children with generations of poverty in their past can enable staff to engage with the critical issues. Discussions like 'X didn't do Y and I don't think it's fair that they get away with it', become 'Why do you think X didn't do Y and how can we avoid it happening again? What solutions can we come up with?'

The theory of self-determination is at play when we look at school leadership and developing staff in this way. Self-determination theory suggests that humans have three universal psychological needs. These needs, according to Dr Edward Deci and other self-determination theory researchers, are not hierarchical or sequential; they are just foundational to us as humans (Ackerman, 2019).

The first of these needs is autonomy: the knowledge that what you are doing is of your own volition and the experience of being the source of your own actions. Autonomy is promoted when people act because they choose to, not because they feel they have to.

The second of these foundational needs is relatedness. Relatedness is people's need to care about and be cared about by other people. In a school setting in which the priority is the experience of young people, establishing mechanisms for people to connect to their feelings about the 'nobler cause' of the work is helpful. Creating opportunities for staff to navigate the complexities of supporting children experiencing poverty provides a basis for discussions that serve to amplify our collective 'why'.

The final of the foundational needs, according to self-determination theorists, is competence. Competence is feeling effective and able. Providing opportunities for staff to feel high levels of competence by involving them in decision-making is not only motivating but also develops their awareness of their own abilities and progress.

Providing opportunities for these three foundational needs to be met in schools can clearly contribute to both wellbeing and the performance of staff. Thus, finding opportunities to cultivate autonomy, relatedness and competence, it could be argued, are wholly valid school CPD priorities.

*

This chapter has explored a number of means of developing staff, from building their resilience and their ability to have challenging conversations through to giving them opportunities to coach and be coached. It has provided some guidance to schools who may not have the financial resources to support expensive training but who could make use of cheaper in-house options such as mentoring or work shadowing. Finally, it has considered the extent to which nurturing autonomy can be an incredibly powerful mechanism for developing people.

Key questions to help you light the way

1. Are you comfortable sitting in the fire with the emotions of your team?
2. Can you find peace with having 'difficult conversations'?
3. Can you find opportunities to develop your staff through coaching?
4. Have you considered the full range of opportunities you have at your disposal to develop your team?
5. How can you use autonomy as a means of creating a staff team with agency and engagement?
6. How can we encourage every leader to demonstrate the courage and integrity to 'sit in the fire' with colleagues in times of challenge? How can you light the way towards this?

8 Leading people with kindness

Chapter overview

This chapter sets out how to be a compassionate leader. It considers the benefits of compassionate leadership and then offers some guidance for leaders wanting to cultivate compassion. The chapter moves on to explore compassionate leadership in action as well as how to develop a compassionate school culture and teach compassion to children. Why? Because compassion is vital as we light the way from our current reality and towards another. Leaders need to be able to show empathy for the present situation and recognise the challenge of change and growth.

In a piece published in the *Harvard Business Review* called 'Why leaders should be mindful, selfless, and compassionate' (Dalai Lama and Hougaard, 2019), the Dalai Lama describes three styles of compassionate leadership. These are: 'the trailblazer who leads from the front, takes risks, and sets an example; the ferryman, who accompanies those in his care and shapes the ups and downs of the crossing; and the shepherd, who sees every one of his flock into safety before himself'. What unites these styles of leadership is that the other person is looked after first.

This chapter will now explore the value of compassionate leadership in schools and explore how compassion can be developed.

What is compassion?

Often confused with empathy, compassion is the ability to understand the way another person is feeling twinned with a strong desire and motivation to alleviate or reduce their suffering. Compassion has, therefore, an active quality that is often overlooked or misunderstood. Compassion is often triggered by noticing the suffering of another human being, experiencing a reaction to it and then wanting to do something about it. However, compassion does not always fit neatly into the way that schools and other organisations are run.

In a study, 'The transformative potential of compassion at work' (Dutton et al., 2005), the authors argue that compassion is 'typically invisible or devalued in work organisations'. While this may be less true of schools, their suggestion that this is because organisations can 'enable or disable compassion by facilitating or hindering the noticing, feeling and responding to pain of their members' is undoubtedly true. As leaders, we have the opportunity to cultivate compassion through being very active about facilitating noticing, feeling and responding, and our ability to do this could have a profound impact on our schools and school communities.

The benefits of compassionate leadership

Leading a school compassionately can have a number of significant benefits, including the following.

Trust

According to Dutton et al. (2005), compassion between people in organisations 'increases levels of interpersonal trust'. Indeed, I have witnessed first-hand the power of compassion in my own leadership when what I would consider a routinely humane way of treating someone has been met with such delight and gratitude that it forever changed our relationship and imbued it with a deep sense of trust come what may!

Quality of connection

Compassion can have an effect on the types of bonds individuals form with each other and can enhance these relationships significantly.

Positive emotion

Both those witnessing compassionate acts in the workplace and those being the recipient of compassion experience high levels of positive emotion. This can lead to a higher degree of productivity and a potential impact on overall improvements in health (Poorkavoos, 2016).

Compassion is self-generating

According to the research (Poorkavoos, 2016), witnessing or experiencing compassion can, in turn, inspire others to act compassionately towards their peers, the result being compassion breeding compassion.

Where to begin

Before thinking of ways in which to develop more compassionate organisations and cultures, it can be a useful practice to get used to direct compassion towards oneself in the first instance. When one scrolls through the EduTwitter feed and witnesses the amount of self-flagellation and denigration going on at our own hands, one realises the power that a sprinkling of self-compassion could have for our workforce.

Dr Kristen Neff, author of a book entitled *Self Compassion*, explains that there are three critical components of self-compassion. These are:

1. Self-kindness vs self-judgment: This is the ability to be warm, friendly and understanding with ourselves as much as we would be with a friend.

2. Common humanity vs isolation: This is recognising that our experience is much more universal than we believe it to be. In other words, recognising that our suffering of failure is a part of the human experience.

3. Mindfulness vs over-identification: Self-compassion requires us to try to maintain some sense of perspective when we are feeling negative rather than obsess about the detail of what we think we have done wrong.

If we can master self-compassion, then it ought to be far easier, as leaders, to learn and begin to cultivate compassion for others we come into contact with.

Becoming a compassionate leader

In his research paper, 'Compassionate leadership: What is it and do organisations need more of it?', Meysam Poorkavoos (2016), sets out a model for compassion in the workplace. The model integrates five aspects of compassion:

1. being alive to the suffering of others

2. being non-judgemental

3. tolerating personal distress

4. being empathetic

5. taking appropriate action.

These are worth illustrating in terms of their relevance to school leadership.

1. Being alive to the suffering of others

The first aspect is a sensitivity to the wellbeing of other people and the ability to be so well attuned to them that you can notice when others are suffering or in need.

I believe the ability to be alive to others is a fundamental leadership skill. In busy schools, with tight deadlines and competing demands, there is a relentlessness to the volume of work that leaders are usually responsible for driving. Often this means keeping a steady and consistent pressure around the meeting of deadlines and accountabilities as well as being able to challenge people when responsibilities are not being discharged. Sometimes the insistence of the pace and volume of work serves to exacerbate what might already be a challenging time for a staff member. Being alive to the suffering of others requires that we are able to offer a full about-turn if necessary and change the course of work and pressure for members of our team.

2. Being non-judgemental

According to Poorkavoos, the ability to be non-judgemental is a huge part of being a compassionate leader. Compassionate leaders need to be able to accept and validate the person suffering and not judge them. Indeed, what Poorkavoos identifies is that judging people when they are going through pain is one of the obstacles to compassion itself in that it blocks our ability to feel and see things from the other's perspective.

The ability to be non-judgemental can be challenging in a school context when it comes to managing severe breaches in the workplace. However, there is a place for dealing with professional misconduct compassionately.

Most school leaders will inevitably face situations involving gross misconduct. These are occasions when a member of staff has committed theft or fraud, or when there has been an instance of serious insubordination, a serious breach of health and safety or an instance of discrimination or harassment, for example.

Leading people with kindness

In any of these situations, you will be guided by your HR advisors as to the appropriate course of action, which could lead you towards either a final written warning, demotion or dismissal. In these situations, one is usually so disappointed that a member of their staff has behaved in this way that it can be challenging to maintain objectivity and clarity. However, it is in these moments that your leadership will truly be felt and you will be able to look back on the way you have handled it with confidence that you were every bit the ethical and compassionate leader.

I recall vividly the occasion on which this level of steady objectivity and compassion was required of me. I was a headteacher and found myself managing a case of serious misconduct. For much of the time, I was in complete shock. I was saddened on behalf of the members of my team who had supported this person in times of need. I was devastated for us all, as we had all had our trust broken. The shock soon turned to anger as I realised the extent of the breach of professional standards. I had to make a conscious decision not to turn that anger into judgement and contempt of the person involved. I quickly saw that bearing a grudge against this person was going to turn inward on me and would mean I was no longer showing up as the kind of leader I want to be.

During my management of this case, I actively chose non-judgement, and it made all the difference. With years between me and that situation, I genuinely believe that a compassionate, non-judgemental and professional approach to dealing with the case and the person was the perfect course of action.

3. Tolerating personal distress

Poorkavoos describes distress tolerance as 'the ability to bear or hold difficult emotions'. This is a particular skill that is, for some unknown reason, entirely left off the curriculum when it comes to leadership development programmes.

A school leader who cannot tolerate the distress of others is in the wrong line of work. A senior leader who shuts down when people break down in tears or who feels discomfort when someone hits hard times and therefore cannot respond appropriately causes immeasurable damage to the sufferer.

Indeed, those who, because of their lack of tolerance, make no space for distress to be properly manifested and contained in the workplace push the suffering back onto the sufferer and fail to make the most of situations that bind us together as we are reminded of our collective humanity.

Accommodating the personal lives of staff can be an area that school leaders find tricky. Over the years, I have had many conversations with staff who have encountered, in their moment of need, leaders who have found it difficult to respond with the sensitivity, calm and reassurance of a human capable of holding space for others.

This is a skill that can be developed, however, and it is my hope that some of the strategies for developing a sense of self outlined in Chapter 5, page 48, will support leaders in developing the skills of holding space in the face of crisis, trauma or distress.

4. Being empathetic

Empathy involves understanding the emotions of another person. Most of us are equipped to demonstrate empathy with our family members, friends and loved ones. If seen as a skill that can be developed in the workplace, turning to team members and looking at them as part of your extended family can be a good starting point.

5. Taking appropriate action

When we can begin to view others empathetically, we can begin to ask ourselves what the right course of action might be, even if it's not the easy course of action.

Taking the right course of action, according to Poorkavoos, comes when we have taken efforts to really get to know the person. It is worth noting that the easy course of action may be to let others handle a situation. So, for example, leaders can find themselves leaning on HR or less senior members of staff to deal with staffing issues or challenging situations involving a member of staff in their personal life.

I would say that, in almost all cases, it is good for the headteacher to get to know the person involved and seek to personally ensure that they do the right thing for that member of staff. Posing the question 'What would Gandhi do in this situation?' or 'How would the Buddha have dealt with this?' I find to be a handy prompt when I am trying to find a more universal sense of 'rightness'!

Compassionate leadership in action

We can learn the skills of compassion, and we can try to cultivate these as leaders, using them whenever we have the opportunity. However, being a compassionate leader is as much about knowing how to use these skills as it is about creating a culture in which all people are invited and inspired to act compassionately.

The school culture that emerges under the compassionate leader is one in which supporting and helping colleagues is celebrated. It is likely to be a culture in which there is a high tolerance for the complexities and challenges of individuals' lives. It is also likely to be a culture in which the infrastructure supports collegiality and support between colleagues.

Leaders need to be at the front when it comes to modelling compassion, which means they need to put themselves regularly in the position of calling out for a compassionate response. Compassion breeds compassion and, as leaders, we must have faith and unshakeable confidence in the culture we are creating, knowing that we can trust that compassion will come our way when we need it. As Poorkavoos points out, 'Leaders can act as role models and support the compassion process by expressing care and concern towards their team members. They can also encourage a culture of openness by sharing their own problems, signalling that it is appropriate to talk about personal difficulties.'

Poorkavoos sets out some helpful questions for leaders to help them identify some of the activities that can foster compassion in work. I have adapted these below so they are specific to school leaders.

1. Does your school promote a culture in which people trust each other and know that if they need to talk about their problems, other team members won't judge them but will try to help? Have you safeguarded against a gossip culture and do you have a low tolerance for it?

2. Does your school encourage others to respond to a colleague's suffering? Sometimes people feel they need to wait for permission to support others in the workplace. In other situations, they want reassurance that their proposed action is appropriate.

3. Do you as a school leader show care and concern towards people in your team? Are you the kind of leader who knows what is going on in the lives of your immediate team members? Remember what they are juggling outside of work and show an interest in how they are coping.

4. Do you as a school leader understand the value of sharing problems with others? Do you trust that if you open up you will be met with compassion? Do you model being open to compassion by asking for it to be shown to you?

5. Do the people in your direct team know that you will try to help them if they have a problem? Do you have an open door and a curiosity towards helping solve seemingly intractable problems?

6. Are your school staff in regular close contact (for example, through face-to-face daily or weekly department meetings)? Have you made sure that there are structures that support connection and that all members of staff have opportunities to be noticed and checked in on?

7. Are there strong connections between people in teams across the school, which make staff feel seen, felt, known and not alone? Have you ensured that the infrastructure supports collegiality, from the environment of staff and workrooms through to the way that meetings are structured and organised?

8. When people in school notice a change in the way a team member is showing up to school, do they feel comfortable about inquiring further?

9. Have you created a school culture in which it is the norm to ask about feelings and emotions? As a school leader, you will need to model this from the front.

10. Does it feel normal in your school for staff to know about each other's lives and pay attention to the pain and suffering of a colleague? Have you created a school culture that is robust and resilient when pain is present by exploring these issues as they arise and confronting bereavement, grief or other painful life circumstances with openness and compassion?

11. Do staff in your school feel safe in sharing their personal problems, issues and challenges with each other? Have you ensured that the way you hold space for people means they are assured of confidentiality and that they understand that further action is by way of supporting them?

12. Do staff in your school feel they can openly express their emotional pain? Have you created a school coaching culture that is fearless in the face of emotion? This container will not only support school staff but will pay dividends when it comes to staff managing and holding the emotions of the children.

How to cultivate a compassionate school culture

Compassionate school culture can be built top-down, with the headteacher and school leaders modelling it. It can also be built from the bottom up, with compassion being activated on a daily basis in classrooms and on the playground.

Often the desire to remind children about the need for compassion comes up when there has been some incident involving unkindness towards others in the school community and occasionally beyond the school community. If the following suggestions about how to teach compassion are followed and properly embedded, through a pastoral programme that supports a return on a cyclical basis to these ideas, it will help your students immeasurably.

Language of compassion

One of the most helpful things I have encountered while thinking through how to teach children about compassion is to help them in their familiarity with using the language of compassion. An activity involving asking children (depending on their age) to try to define or research the meaning of the following words can support this:

- philanthropy
- generosity
- empathy
- mercy
- benevolence
- kindness
- humanity
- understanding
- sympathy.

This activity can then be expanded to encourage children to consider the themes of the current book they are reading. Explore whether or not any of these themes appear. Similarly, scanning the recent newspapers and trying to find usage of the words they have researched can support children in beginning to find evidence of the existence of compassion all around them.

Why should we be compassionate?

It is worth discussing with children when and where being compassionate might be useful or even necessary. Compassion needs context and children need opportunities to explore what kinds of context would make them feel not just that they empathised with the person involved but that they wanted to help the person involved actively.

Compassion is always hardest to elicit when you don't feel sympathy towards the other person, as it makes it harder to act for the other when there is no sympathy. Understanding the difference that being compassionate can make will enable young people to choose it, even when they do not feel compelled to in the first instance. Practising compassion takes time but, in my experience, the more you practise it, the more readily available it is.

It is also inspiring and motivating for children to be reminded that compassion breeds compassion, and so being compassionate will have a positive impact on those around you and will extend out towards those you don't even know.

Discuss suffering and enable the noticing of suffering for others

In the times we are living in, with distress and trauma being broadcast into most living rooms daily, it can be difficult for some people to maintain their sense of compassion. The stress associated with dealing with the trauma of others is known as compassion fatigue. For young people, the sheer scale of human suffering could be potentially overwhelming, so what teachers need to do is to bring it down to a more manageable scale. Asking children to think about who they would want to help if they could and asking them to consider what concerns them about the suffering they have witnessed will help them.

Being compassionate with ourselves

This next exercise is not one I have tried but I love the idea of it. It asks children to write a love letter to themselves. The first thing they should do is to try to identify something about themselves that they don't particularly like or something about their behaviour that they give themselves a hard time about.

Once this has been identified, they should write it down and try to describe how this thing makes them feel. The next step is to begin to craft a letter in which they express kindness, compassion and understanding for this thing.

It is really hard to do this (I know from personal experience), but the key is to ask children to imagine they are writing from the perspective of someone who really, really cares for them and who would forgive them anything.

This activity could be immensely powerful. Self-compassion is even more challenging for many of us than demonstrating compassion for absolute strangers. After undertaking an exercise like this, allow students space and time to come and talk to an adult if they need to.

Everyday compassion in the home

I was recently in a discussion with a headteacher in which we talked about some of the challenges of leading an inclusive school. In particular, we talked about the situation that can arise when one parent demands actions on behalf of their child and the action they demand will result in the exclusion of another child. This comes up when, for example, one child's behaviour regularly threatens the peace and ability to learn of others. Our discussion led us to consider whether or not some parents felt that this kind of action was the best means of protecting their child.

We wondered whether in fact teaching children to be compassionate in the face of challenging situations might be more helpful. This, we surmised, would give them a tool that they could use to tackle virtually any situation in a way that merely excluding another human being does not.

We talked about the fact that while each child is born with the ability to show compassion, this compassion needs to be nurtured, and sometimes families need guidance on how to cultivate compassion in their children.

Here are a few ideas that headteachers and leaders can insert into bulletins or newsletters to support parents in their nurturing of compassion at home.

1. Encouraging empathy for other children

A straightforward exercise that can be used in the home is to encourage empathy for other children. When challenge or conflict arises in school with friends and classmates, it can be helpful for parents to adopt a neutral stance (however hard that is).

For parents to ask their children to consider the challenge or conflict from the perspective of the other child is powerful and allows the child a moment to put themselves in someone else's shoes and nurture compassion.

2. Noticing compassion

Noticing compassion can be quite a simple and effective means of parents supporting their children. When reading stories together or observing the actions of characters (real or imagined), it helps for parents to call out the compassionate deed, stating how that deed is likely to have had an impact on the other or the world.

3. Household chores

Household chores can, in part, be about parents instilling a sense of communal responsibility in their children. However, another aspect of ensuring that children undertake household chores is to teach them an understanding of the needs of others. Cleaning the bathroom or the car encourages children to recognise the pleasure someone else will feel as a consequence of their actions.

Being compassionate within the class

Our school rules tend to determine how students behave. However, alongside the conduct that we expect from every member of the school community, there are other opportunities to nurture conduct implicitly through encouraging compassion.

In one school I worked in, one of our NQTs started the year with a 'Compassion Book' (I have seen others make this into a notice board). As part of the class's PSHE curriculum, the children would make active use of the book. They would call others out for compassionate conduct and write letters to classmates to show appreciation for them. These letters would all go in the book, and they would be read out periodically. Compassionate behaviour in school and outside of school was recognised, and children would be encouraged to write about their own compassionate acts and add these to the book too.

In the same school, it was standard practice for teachers to shake the hands of children at the beginning of the day and at the end of the day. Now, many of us have seen the endless hug-a-thons on Facebook as class teachers allow children to opt for a handshake or hug. What I have witnessed to be true is that children hugely value being seen, witnessed and physically recognised in this way. Indeed, when we once had a teacher who was sloppy about this practice and had started the year shaking hands with the children and then partway through the year just stopped, the children were outraged and this was their primary complaint about him. A simple handshake may not feel like a significant act of compassion, but it is a profound recognition of the other and can be usefully integrated into the classroom.

Children are fantastic at helping each other out. One of the schools I worked with recently had children available in the playground to support those children who didn't have anyone to play with during playtime. The children proudly wore red sashes and sat on a special bench in the playground so that they could be available and visible to others. They loved the opportunity to demonstrate compassion for others because it is hard-wired in us.

*

This chapter has explored the ways in which using compassion in schools can benefit the school community and enhance leadership. It considered self-compassion before moving on to look at how school leaders can create compassionate school environments for staff. Finally, it has discussed the benefits of teaching compassion to children.

Key questions to help you light the way

1. How comfortable are you at showing compassion with your team?
2. How able are you to hold the space for a person in crisis?
3. How do you model compassionate leadership?
4. How are you teaching compassion in the classroom?
5. How are you supporting parents in introducing compassion into the home?
6. How can we ensure that compassion is seen as a prerequisite to good leadership? How can you light the way towards this?

9 Working through crisis

Chapter overview

This chapter sets out how to manage a crisis in a way that supports every member of the school community. It demonstrates that there is always personal growth involved in managing crisis and it argues for good planning to mitigate the effects of crisis if it should arise. Why? Because when lighting the way in challenging times, crisis is almost inevitable. Leaders must have the confidence to manage crisis in order that its impacts are lessened for members of the community.

Inevitably, in our schools, bad things sometimes happen. When I look back at the ways I responded to critical incidents in school, I am grateful that I had done some serious inner work and was confident enough in my leadership to trust that I would handle things with integrity.

That said, looking back I do feel there were opportunities to have been better prepared in ways that would underscore the school's values and ensure that everyone in a leadership role was confident of their part in managing the difficulty. By this, I mean that on reflection the expectation was (rightly) that I would set the tone and make decisions rather than there being a confidence that decisions would be made by following a code that determined everything we did in the school.

Critical incident management is often presented as a risk to schools, with a focus on the business angle. Schools and trusts are more aware than ever about the 'reputational damage' that critical incidents can present schools with. There are, however, many more far-reaching reasons why leaders should think through how their school will respond to a crisis.

The most important outcome that careful planning around critical incidents can create is that staff and students are left with a deep sense of safety. Staff should feel that leaders know what to do, that leaders can be trusted and that their faith in leadership has been rightly given. The planning of how a school responds to critical incidents ought to be given as much thought as the ways in which it responds to praise, positive student events and a great set of examination results.

What constitutes a critical incident?

Thankfully, serious in-school incidents resulting in the death or harm of children and staff are very rare in the UK. There is a lack of recent data, but according to the English Outdoor Council's 2010 report 'Nothing ventured: Balancing risk and benefits in the outdoors' (Gill, 2010), the likelihood of a fatality on a school trip is about the same as in everyday life. Their summary is that 'on a typical school visit, the children who take part are at no greater risk of death than their schoolmates who have stayed behind'.

That said, there are a number of incidents that occur in schools on a daily basis that could and often do become critical incidents.

According to a BBC investigation, in 2014 'a total of 30,394 crimes were reported at primary schools, secondary schools and further education establishments – excluding universities' (Beckford, 2015). The *Telegraph* reported earlier this year that in 2018 alone 'more than 50 ten and eleven-year-olds were convicted or cautioned for knife crime' (Hymas, 2019). The report continues that overall statistics for the number of ten- to 17-year-olds 'convicted or cautioned for knife crime is at a ten-year high, up by 62 per cent to 4,103 offenders in just five years'.

In their guide to managing critical incidents in school, the Northern Ireland Department of Education describes a critical incident as 'any sudden and unexpected incident or sequence of events which causes trauma within a school community and which overwhelms the normal coping mechanisms of that school'.

Critical elements obviously include the very worst cases of death or serious injury within school. Indeed, they include anything that is of a high media profile, for example the presence of firearms or weapons in school as well as the identification of a procedural failure or poor decision-making in dealing with incidents.

Some critical elements that will be very familiar to many school leaders are those such as the continued or worsening situation in relation to a vulnerable child or an incident motivated or exacerbated by race, faith, gender, sexual orientation, disability or other factors. Likewise, tensions rising in the school or in the local community, situations when a student is a repeat victim of crime or where crime keeps happening in a particular place, or breakdowns in the relationship between school, family or students and thus a loss of confidence all constitute critical elements.

Other critical elements include situations where there is nothing as a leader that you can do, for example in the case of worsening natural causes, such as flood water deepening.

It is worth noting that schools are not expected to deal with critical incidents on their own and, depending on the nature of the incident, multi-agency responses or simply the support of your CEO or local authority might be needed.

How would you respond?

Many school leaders will be familiar with the development of issues that have escalated to the point of becoming critical incidents. It is for this reason that I believe time spent dwelling as a leadership team on what the school's response to the afore-mentioned list might be is as valuable as time spent mapping the school's lockdown and emergency procedures.

Take, for example, the familiar situation of the 'vulnerability of a young person due to mental health'. This is a widespread occurrence. Most schools have several students who match this profile. Time spent with the SLT thinking through the potential escalation of a situation involving this young person could prove to be time well spent. This time could safeguard the wellbeing of this child, and it will engender trust from the wider school community if the school ever needs to move into a planned and well-thought-through response to an incident.

On one occasion, and thus one occasion too many, I was leading in a school in which a young person who was already being monitored by the pastoral team took a handful of pharmaceutical drugs. Sadly, this is a rising issue for schools across the country. According to a 2018 *Guardian* report, an NHS-funded study found that between 1998 and 2014 there was 'A threefold to fourfold leap in people aged 10 to 25 being poisoned by antidepressants. A trebling in those who needed medical treatment after taking too much aspirin or anti-inflammatory drugs, such as ibuprofen. A threefold rise in females poisoned by paracetamol.' (Campbell, 2018) My team responded with calm; they were composed and professional. We worked through the day supporting the young person and getting her the medical help she needed and supporting other students affected by the incident.

I ended up accompanying the young person to the hospital and then supporting her parents with the implications of what had happened. Members of my senior team worked with me well into the night to ensure that communications to the wider parent body were clear and demonstrated the school's commitment to wellbeing and safety. In the following days and weeks, we kept up our regular communications with all affected parties.

However, we could have done better.

In acknowledging the rising number of students in our school who were talking with members of our pastoral team about their mental health and disclosing a familiarity with drugs and alcohol, we'd adapted our PSHE programmes. We'd held parents' evenings on the topics that were being raised in school and that concerned us, such as the increasing number of children talking about getting access to drugs and alcohol outside of school. We'd invited in mental health professionals to lead parent workshops on supporting their children with mental health. Our pastoral team had kept excellent records, there were strategies in place to support children whose behaviour was escalating, and we'd discussed the issues in staff meetings at all levels.

But, when it came to the worst-case scenario and the afore-mentioned incident unfolded, I hadn't predicted the school's exact response. Indeed, we had the generic response to serious incidents but, on reflection, this could have been far more.

Taking our planning through to the final stages – namely including in our strategy for supporting children with mental health and wellbeing a set of guidance for what happens when the worst thing happens – would have led to a greater sense of confidence and ease with our procedures as the events unfolded.

Keeping your values intact

As I've mentioned previously, an incident involving a serious degree of vandalism to one of the schools I worked in was much publicised at the time and then many months later. I received a call in the early hours from my deputy headteacher, who was on site as he had received a call from our site manager. A significant amount of graffiti had been sprayed across the school. It was graffiti of the very worst kind: offensive comments about members of staff and hugely distasteful imagery.

There was absolutely no way that I was going to allow students on site to witness the offensive language and no way I was going to subject staff who had been mentioned in the graffiti to the humiliation of having students getting sight of it, so we made a very early decision to close the school.

It was a rural school, so it meant that staff had to turn buses around that it had been too late to cancel. The whole team pitched up to the school gates to let parents who were dropping their children off know that the school was closed for the day.

I've never been more grateful to be part of a supportive trust, as it was my CEO who came to the rescue and managed the inevitable press interest. But we were being filmed at the time as part of a BBC documentary, and it was in my reflections with the producers about the incident that I was able to articulate my values of integrity, fairness and compassion and be thankful that every day, no matter the situation, I had an opportunity to live in accordance with them.

Anatomy of a critical incident by Lisa Howell, headteacher

Leading a school inevitably involves leading staff and students through 'ordinary everyday emergencies'. I discussed this aspect of leadership at my headteacher interview. However, it also involves, on rare occasions, leading others through extraordinary, not-so-everyday emergencies and sometimes through a crisis.

Whether you have prepared for headship through courses such as the National Professional Qualification for Headship (NPQH) or simply by thinking about and planning for such moments, three things have become clear to me. Firstly, no matter what eventualities you believe you have mentally rehearsed, the actuality, the complexity and indeed the timing of such events can never fully be anticipated. My wise deputy head once said to me that 'headship is as much about common sense, leadership and temperament as anything else'. I tend to agree, but I also believe that a strong sense of ethical leadership and honesty are vital.

Incidents involving knives, while not 'everyday', are increasingly prevalent. Thus, one Friday afternoon – it is always a Friday – I was informed that one such incident had just been played out at our school gates. No one was injured, and the knife had been secured by a member of staff. At this point, I fully realised just how much staff look for a leader. A moment such as this is a moment when, whatever your preferred leadership style (also something I had discussed at interview), it needs to flex. As a primary school colleague once said, 'the moment when a downpour occurs just before break and your staff want to know whether this is a "wet break" is not the moment for a coaching conversation. Yet, neither is this the time to exclude colleagues whose opinions and expertise you value. Yes, you need to show calm, measured and decisive leadership, but given that your team will become the leaders of tomorrow, it would also seem a moment to include them.'

For me, communication is key. When the knife incident happened at my school, my first call was to ensure students and staff were safe, my second was to call the police, and my third was the briefest of calls home to my long-suffering partner to explain that I would be 'as long as it takes' and to ask him to postpone our social plans. This enabled me to metaphorically 'clear my desk' and give the situation my fullest attention.

As well as securing the safety of all involved, I needed time to do the right thing by students, their parents and our staff. I always ask myself what I would expect, and more importantly want, from a headteacher in these circumstances. As a student I would want reassurance; as a parent I would want to know what had been done and what was being done to ensure that my child's safety – and that of the other students – was paramount; as a member of staff I would want to know what had happened, what was being done for the students, how I should respond to any questions directed at me and what was being done for my own safety.

So, before I left, I ensured that the team had done all of this. This involved a core team with specific roles and a wider team who were informed of the outline of events and asked to support the core team. It involved phone calls home to parents of those directly involved. It also involved a careful communication home to all parents and an email to all staff. Finally, I informed my chair of governors and the CEO of the MAT.

It was these actions that stood us in good stead as the not-so-everyday, not-so-ordinary emergency escalated over the weekend into a full-blown crisis.

For, although students and parents were happy with the actions we had taken and felt fully supported, we live in an age of social media. The youngster who wielded the knife was not actually one of our students: he attended the pupil referral unit (PRU) less than a mile away and had visited our school gates as he had a 'beef' with one of our students. The incident, perhaps inevitably, had been filmed, shared and gone 'viral'. Thus, I awoke on Monday morning to a full-page tabloid picture, headline and media link featuring our school. At this point, the fact that I had been open and honest, sharing details with all concerned, particularly parents, reaped benefits.

The team met early. I reiterated roles, including those of the wider team supporting those at the centre. A list of jobs and responsibilities was created, but it was me, as leader, who undertook responsibility for that list, including the 'completed' column, to ensure that during the often-frenetic business of running a school nothing was overlooked due to general busyness. I also checked that staff felt able and supported to carry out these tasks, offering them the chance to rehearse conversations if they felt that would be useful. Again, it felt important to delegate, but also to support, and as headteacher to retain overall responsibility. People perform much better when they know they are supported and know that someone has their back! It is also, however, important to remember that your team are the leaders of tomorrow. Too often, as a member of SLT in the past, I had felt excluded from such moments. Your team needs to support but also to learn at such times.

By 8:45 am, a further message had been sent to parents, a PowerPoint to reassure students had been prepared for all tutors to use during tutor time, and I stood in front of the staff at an emergency briefing. I had also reassured the staff that the emergency briefing did not concern Ofsted – just to keep a sense of perspective. Humour always needs to be carefully used, but holding up a tabloid paper featuring our school as a central part of 'Knife-crime Britain' afforded a moment for some carefully and appropriately judged lightness, quickly followed by a clear explanation of what had happened, what was being done and what the staff's roles were – to guide nervous youngsters by using the prepared PowerPoint, to reassure students and a plea to help out with extra visibility at the school gates. As ever, my staff responded brilliantly – because we were a team with a central aim and a central vision, and because 'care' sat at the centre of all we did.

It is a testament to this calm and thorough approach and to placing honest communication at the centre of decision-making that I only had two phone calls from concerned parents. I dealt with these personally, because I would have wanted to speak with the headteacher. Staff really stepped up and those staff involved in the initial incident were allowed time for a lengthy debrief with me – because if this had happened to me, again I would have wanted to talk to the head – and were offered access to counsellors.

Something else struck me as the day played out. Although only two parents called in, we were inundated with calls from local and national media. Because we had issued statements on our website and had communicated directly with parents, we were able to direct all press enquiries to these sources. This avoided the 'no comment' or 'the headteacher is unavailable for comment' scenarios, which can be damaging. I felt very strongly that my job was to be in school, accessible and visible to reassure students, parents and staff. I was invited to London to appear on a breakfast show to discuss knife crime in Britain, but politely refused and redirected the media to my CEO. I had asked my staff to help out on the school gates for the coming week to reassure youngsters and their parents; it would have been morally wrong not to be there with them.

An educational blog I read following the incident gave advice to headteachers facing a crisis. Two things really resonated. Firstly, up until this moment, you have dealt with everything that has come your way, and this will be no different. Secondly, 'this too will pass'. But it was actually the words of Angie Browne that went through my mind that weekend: 'You have to tell yourself that you can steer this ship.' And we did!

In social care, the use of supervision is central. I hope it will be the case in education in the near future. For now, I simply make sure that I have my fellow leaders near, and their numbers firmly in my phone. On being appointed, a colleague who was a few years into headship said to me, 'If you ever need to close your door and call to talk through a problem – just call.' Leading can feel lonely at certain moments. However great and loyal your team are, some situations require you to stand firm and shoulder the burden. Staying calm, trusting those you work with but ultimately asking yourself the question, 'What would I want a headteacher to do if this was the school my child attended, or the school where I taught?' has served me well so far.

The case study above underscores the importance of 'keeping your head when all about are losing theirs'. The incident reaching the tabloid front covers bears this out. What is also helpful about this example is that it highlights the potential for escalation from an incident with critical elements to a critical incident. Here the critical element was a young person with a weapon, and the escalation occurred because it became of public interest, such is the intertwined nature of young people and social media.

However, much as we may not like this age of social media, managing the media is an essential part of handling difficult situations. Getting prepared ahead of time for critical incidents like these and planning your school's execution of duties may not seem like an urgent priority now, but it will pay you back in dividends.

Dealing with critical incidents

From my own experiences, I know how important it is for school leaders to plan for critical incidents. The following sections will offer some practical advice on how to be prepared in case an incident occurs.

Develop a policy

It is really important that school leaders know what they would do and how they would intend to handle an unfortunate situation if one occurred. A policy will help you work with your team to set this out.

The policy should identify the Emergency Plan and should set out the Critical Incident Team, namely who would deal with critical incidents and what their roles and responsibilities would be in the event of an incident. The policy should also include a list of agencies and support staff at local authority or trust level that you will need to contact in the event of an emergency. The policy needs to be updated on a regular basis and must take account of changes to personnel.

Use the curriculum

The school's PSHE curriculum is the place to ensure that young people have explored topics such as loss and bereavement and it is the place to develop skills that support them to manage change, difficult emotions and challenging situations. There is no way you can truly prepare students for the fallout of a critical incident but you can make sure that challenging issues are addressed cyclically and that the school curriculum does not shy away from these difficult topics.

The Emergency Plan

Schools and trusts will all have their own guidance on the format and steps of an emergency plan but most should include the following:

- Gather information and assess the situation.
- Ensure safety of students and staff.
- Call the emergency services if required and administer first aid if necessary.
- Appraise your critical incident team and reaffirm roles and responsibilities.

- If the incident has happened off-site, establish your police liaison.

- Notify your trust, local authority and governors.

- Contact the parents of those involved in the incident.

- Determine the protocols for wider information sharing.

- Over the next 24 to 72 hours, hold meetings for students and parents and provide daily briefings and updates for staff.

- Provide individual pastoral support for staff and students.

Look after yourself

We all know and understand the references to putting your oxygen mask on first. In the case of dealing with the aftermath of a critical incident, it is important that you look after yourself in order that you can focus your attentions on those around you. Be aware of the things that have supported you when dealing with trauma in the past and use these strategies or tools. Whatever you do, don't underplay the impact that overseeing a critical incident can have. Look after yourself, eat good food, rest and let family and friends be there for you.

When I talk to future school leaders about their preparedness for headship, the one consistent barrier is their fear of having to manage a critical incident. I doubt there is a headteacher in the land who feels that, when the moment came that they needed to manage an emergency, everything went as well as it could have done. However, there will be many who can attest that being prepared helped them hugely and that knowing they could weather storms of that nature deepened their confidence in themselves and their leadership.

*

This chapter has looked at some of the ways in which managing critical incidents can help deepen your sense of self as a leader and give others confidence in your leadership. It has examined what critical incidents are, provided a detailed case study of a critical incident and set out how leaders can better prepare themselves to manage critical incidents.

1. How well prepared is your school to manage critical incidents?
2. How have you reflected on your management of challenging situations and incorporated your learning into plans for the future?
3. How confident are you in leading your team through a critical incident?
4. How confident are you in managing the media?
5. How confident are you in managing the fallout of critical incidents in school and on social networks?
6. How can we embrace the likelihood of crisis in the full knowledge that, as leaders, we have the tools and skills to lead people through it? How can you light the way towards this?

PART 4

Leading children with moral purpose

10 Teaching values

Chapter overview

This chapter sets out the need for teaching values in our schools. It sets out the crisis there has been in values-based leadership on the global stage. It suggests some ways of teaching values in the classroom and then explores how to go about revitalising your personal and institutional values. Why? Because to light the way in challenging times leaders must lead with unshakeable confidence in their values.

As we have discussed in the previous chapters on leadership, there does seem to be a schism emerging between the leaders in our society and those they attempt to make follow them. In Machiavelli's view, it doesn't always pay to act virtuously when you are surrounded by those who are not; rather, if you want to lead you must be able to use virtue when it is needed and be prepared not to use it at all. This seems to be an approach that resonates with many of today's world leaders, and it appears to be at odds with the majority of people who still believe that leaders should be virtuous, morally upstanding and own a 'true' set of values.

The Ipsos MORI Veracity Index has since 1983 run a poll to discover how trusted various professions are in Britain, and it is no surprise to see that trust in politicians is low, with only 16 per cent of those polled trusting them to tell the truth. Aside from advertising executives, politicians were, in 2018, the least trusted group of professionals in the UK (Ipsos, 2018). The fact that our political leaders are the least trusted group in our society says a lot about the correlation many people will draw between leadership and a lack of values. In many ways I believe this means that we need to do even more as school leaders to establish trust from those we work with and those we serve.

Is there a lack of ethical leadership? By Dr Neil Hawkes, Values Based Education

I first became involved in values education because I noticed that there were an increasing number of children coming to school without a basic understanding of words such as respect, tolerance, empathy, trust and friendship. Those who had access to this vocabulary had an advantage, as these children were able to behave well, be truthful, show basic manners, form good relationships, be more reflective and make the most of their schooling. Above all, they had the ability to control their own behaviour and had a strong sense of the difference between right and wrong – they were happier.

As a headteacher, I wanted all children to have access to what I now call an ethical vocabulary, so that none would be disadvantaged and all would want to live the values that they were learning at school. With the support of the school community, I introduced an educational philosophy and practices that would, through values-based education, help children to develop ethical intelligence and be ethical leaders. A part of my philosophy is the understanding that we should all be leaders of our self and, at times, of others in the many roles we play in life. I researched the effects of creating a values-based school, which showed the incredible personal and social impact on children and the school community.

In recent decades the focus of the school curriculum has become fixed on academic standards and attainment, with the emphasis on learning more and more about mathematics and literacy at a younger and younger age. The result in England, as in many countries, is that children are not exposed to a rich, diverse curriculum and are not educated with a sufficient focus on the development of ethical intelligence, which forms ethical leaders. Currently national leaders are not held accountable for the lies they tell, their behaviour or the way they manipulate public opinion to gain power. The general public is often unaware of being exposed to lies and half-lies, whether it is from the media or people with access to power.

What can be done to mitigate the social entropy this creates? I believe an answer is the creation of values-based schools and organisations. In values-based schools, pupils learn about values and more importantly how to live them in their lives by practically putting them into action. They become more aware of their own behaviour and that of others. They learn self-leadership and know how to self-regulate their internal worlds. Adults who model positive human values teach them. Parents become a core part of the process.

Yes, there is a crisis created by a lack of ethical leadership but there is hope, as I believe that schools can play a major role in creating a new generation, who are driven by a keen sense of ethics and the role this plays in our lives and society.

The children we are currently teaching are part of the so-called Generation Z. What we already know about them is that many of them are curious, challenging and questioning the way our leaders execute their leadership.

According to a report published by McKinsey and Company (Francis and Hoefel, 2018), they are influencers and 'true digital natives: from earliest youth, they have been exposed to the internet, to social networks, and to mobile systems'. This generation is used to being bombarded with information and has learned how to handle data and information from multiple sources. That said, this is the generation growing up in the era of fake news, and according to the McKinsey report, this makes them distrustful of traditional structures and institutions.

Generation Z is the generation of Greta Thunberg, and they are unhappy with the lack of ethical practice exhibited by businesses and politics. A search for truth defines them, and so, in these socially fragmented times, we need to support them to sort and sift through information, to discover personal truths and to identify the values they want to live their lives by.

Personal and public values

Our values are the fundamental beliefs that guide us and determine, to a large extent, our attitudes and our actions. They provide us with a route map through challenging situations, as they remind us of the kind of person we have sought to be and therefore indicate what, for us, is the right course of action.

We grow up in families that may or may not have solid values and expectations of how each member of the family should conduct themselves. The absence of strong values in the family will determine behaviour as much as the presence of them.

For some people, cultural or religious values have a considerable part to play in the shaping of their personal value system. If a child grows up in a community that uses the language of values regularly, attends sermons or ceremonies, and is engaged in regular spiritual practice, they tend to carry about an implicit value system.

This means that identifying one's personal values and separating them from a handed-down value system can be a task that doesn't get done. There is a sense for many of us that we have a value system that we were born with and many of us don't check it is still right for us.

Yet one of the most powerful tools I use within my coaching practice is to support coachees in identifying, articulating and then seeking to live by their own values. Coachees are encouraged to question the values they have adopted because they felt it was the right thing to do, and see whether they want to keep hold of them.

In the times in which we are living, with the split we discussed in Chapter 1, page 5, between the very wealthy and the very poor, with the schism between the secular and the spiritual worlds and with the increasing distrust of previously trusted institutions, it is more critical than ever that we give children opportunities to learn about their values. When children know their personal values, they have a chance to change their behaviours and to experience the congruity that comes from acting in accordance with their beliefs.

Exploring personal values with young people

The following exercise will help you begin the process of exploring values with your students. These activities will enable students to consider the values that resonate with them as well as the ones they would like to see living and breathing in the school at large.

1. Values lists – an exploration

Giant values lists can be a little daunting. However, I have found that using values lists or values sorting cards with coaching clients can provide a speedy way into narrowing down that which is really important to them. I would create a list of values and ensure that they are age-appropriate and will be understood by the children in your class. You can then present them as lists or cut them into cards and ask children to spend a short amount of time looking through them. The aim is for them to come up with a reduced pile of values that mean something to them – around 20 would be a good number.

To support the process of sifting through the values and getting down to 20, it is helpful to scaffold the experience with the following prompts:

- Think of the best moment of your life.
  - Why was it so good?
  - Were any of the values you are looking at present in that moment?

- Think of a time when you've been really sad, disappointed or angry.
  - What made this situation so bad?
  - What value was not present in that moment?

- What are the most important things in your life?

- What makes your heart soar?

- What makes you feel like everything is right in the world?

- How do you like other people to behave towards you?

2. Narrowing the lists

The next stage is to ask students to group their 20 or so values. They should put those values that express a similar theme together. A means of scaffolding the grouping and sorting is to ask them to justify their groupings to a peer and explain why they think the values should be organised in this way.

The final stage of narrowing the list is for the students to pick just one or two values from each group. This stage of the exercise is much more about their gut feeling about which of the values is most important to them. It is worth reminding students at this stage that this process of identifying our core values is one that many adults come back to time and time again. If this is the first time they have done this kind of exercise, they need to know their choices are not set in stone but will be the beginnings of creating a personal value system that will develop as they become more attuned to the way in which they want to conduct themselves in the world.

3. Bringing the values to life

The students will now have between four and eight values that they feel are representative of what is most important to them. Now is the chance to bring these to life. They should take each value and explain the following in a short sentence:

- why this value is important in their lives
- how this value influences their behaviour.

One of my most important values is integrity, so I might write:

- Integrity is important to me as there have been times when I have not been entirely truthful, and it has never turned out well.
- I now use integrity in my life to ensure that everything I say will be matched in my behaviour and my actions.

4. Using my values

The final stage of this process is to facilitate students' thinking about how and when they will have an opportunity to live in accordance with their values. Ask students to write down two or three events, challenges or opportunities that are coming up for them. Then ask them to consider for each one how they will have an opportunity to demonstrate one or two of their values in each of those scenarios.

Identifying the values your school needs to focus on

Identifying individual values contributes to the personal development of young people. Being clear about the values that a school holds dear helps everyone within the organisation contribute to a meaningful culture and supports a community code of conduct. The following steps are provided to help you identify values as a whole school community.

1. Use your leadership

While personal values are (obviously) personal, a school's values are, to a large extent, shaped by the leader of the school. Of course, you will need to ensure the engagement of all stakeholders in the distilling of core values. However, what is assumed is that the leader of the organisation is unequivocal about their values and understands the importance of values. Critically, what is also assumed is that the leader is very clear about the school they are leading, its unique context and, therefore, what broad set of values are needed to create the desired culture.

2. Engage your staff

Rather than using a prepared list of 200 values, it can be helpful for the headteacher to lead a discussion in which staff work individually at first to come up with a list of values stimulated by responding to the following questions:

- What is important about our school?
- What makes this school a brilliant place to work in?

When they have completed this activity, they should get into small teams and group similar values together before finally sharing with the entire staff meeting their top three to five values.

These group responses can be distilled down, as there will be common values across the team, and can later be added to the values identified as important by the students.

3. Engage your students

Asking the staff to repeat the above exercise with the students means the essence of the discussion led by the headteacher runs through the exercise. The activity is not a standalone but very much framed within the unique context of your school.

I would suggest that teachers ask the children the same two questions as above but limit the number of responses each child gives to get more quickly to the essence of young people's views. Students don't want to have their time wasted by writing reams of information that is not going to be utilised, so asking them to come up with two to four values each will suffice.

I then suggest that the top values are distilled by class and then possibly by year group, depending on the size of your school. Keeping things brief is likely to lead to more synergy than you might expect.

Once you have the lists from the children, it is then possible to synthesise and distil to reach a core set of values that resonate for the whole school community. Once again, these need to be brought to life and time will need to be put in by students and staff in deciding on how these values will determine the attitudes and conduct exemplified in school life on a day-to-day basis.

Sustaining a values-based culture in school

It is one thing to come up with a set of values, but it is another to ensure that these values are 'lived and not just laminated'. Taking the example of a fictional school that embraces certain values, let's walk through how a school leader could ensure that these values were a living part of the school experience and not just paid lip service.

The Nourished School: an example

The Nourished School, having completed the process outlined above, has now distilled their values down to the following: integrity, ambition and resilience.

Their value statements helpfully unpack what these values mean in the context of their school and add detail to support student conduct, staff behaviour and community expectations of the school. Thus, their set of value statements reads as follows:

Integrity

We treat all members of the school community and beyond with compassion, kindness and respect. We are open-minded and welcoming, and we do not tolerate prejudice of any kind. Our integrity makes a positive difference in the world.

Ambition

We are committed to exploring our passions and interests and determined to fulfil our potential and achieve our goals. Our ambition fuels our curiosity and a spirit of adventure.

Resilience

We know we are worthy and capable of overcoming any challenge. We learn from our successes as well as from our setbacks. Our resilience makes us strong.

The Nourished School's values run through the organisation like a stick of rock, and they make an impact on every aspect of school life. Getting to this point took a lot of work. Indeed, the SLT needed to think through every aspect of school life in detail and consider carefully the ways in which they would expect to see their values manifest across them.

Reception

The way visitors and parents are welcomed into the school sets the tone for how people can be expected to be treated by the people and processes of the school. At the Nourished School, the emphasis on 'integrity' means that the reception staff greet all visitors with respect. The reception area is easy to access; no one is left standing in the cold. The reception allows for a proper greeting, and the reception staff have been trained so that they know the importance of warmth, eye contact and professionalism.

When parents or visitors are upset or distressed, when parents have been invited in for sensitive meetings or when parents have come to collect an angry or rampaging child, parents are treated with compassion and kindness. The reception staff can put themselves in their visitor's shoes, and they recognise that navigating school life can sometimes be tricky.

The reception area itself is always improving. The reception staff put a lot of time into maintaining displays and information for parents. The integrity of the reception staff makes a positive difference for visitors, and for parents in particular, who feel confident to walk into the school knowing that they will be welcomed warmly and signposted helpfully.

School signage and displays

School signage is clear. All members of the school community can make use of it. There is an integrity about how school signage has been considered for people across diverse groups. Thus, signs reflect the languages in the school, from Braille through to Punjabi.

The display areas in the school refer to the school's values. There are numerous examples of the value statements around the school and in prominent places.

The displays in classrooms support the growing resilience of students. In some areas, working walls demonstrate what children are working through. In other areas, displays depict the drafting process of work.

There is a sense of pride in the regularly updated displays. In themselves, they draw attention to the ambition the school has for the children and they capture the detail of children working ambitiously to achieve their goals.

State of the buildings, classrooms and playgrounds

Although the premises are old, they are well looked after and maintained. The site team are a hugely valued group, and the headteacher meets with them every week to talk through areas of the school that are a cause for concern or that need attention. Their attention to detail and their prompt responses come as a result of the integrity they hold and the seriousness with which they view their work in the school.

Cleanliness of toilets and dining areas

Toilets and communal spaces are cleaned on a regular basis throughout the day. Duty staff report incidents quickly so that the site team can get to them swiftly. The focus is on providing a well-cared-for environment for the students, and the commitment to this is full of integrity.

The school has responded to feedback that Year 7 sometimes felt intimidated by older children in toilets at breaktime. Thus, staff are always on duty near toilets at break and lunch to ensure that everyone's wellbeing is assured.

Lunches and food

The school has been ambitious in this area. They were determined that they could offer nutritious and delicious healthy food for students. They pushed back when contractors suggested menus that didn't meet their expectations. Eventually, they found a supplier who did support the ambition for family dining and freshly cooked healthy meals.

The school knows about and is committed to nourishing the children holistically, and they have had to show resilience in the face of parental pressure to allow unhealthy snacks in school and in the face of food contractors who haven't wanted to budge. They stayed the course, and the results mean that leaders can walk through the dining hall at lunchtime with integrity, knowing they have done the right thing.

Parents' evenings

The school has worked hard to build the resilience of children. Parents' evenings were an opportunity for the school to develop this further. It has put time into preparing children for hearing their teachers talk with their parents about how they are doing in class and has put time into scaffolding their engagement in these conversations.

Because resilience is so essential to the school, leaders also took steps to reassure parents that they work with students on building resilience and that it is a two-way street. In other words, parents know that teachers are open to constructive feedback. The school helpfully sent out some prompts to support children who may also need to say things to their teacher that they may not have the confidence to do on their own, but that parents' evening and the support of their parents could facilitate.

School meetings

Staff meetings are regular, but they do not waste people's time. The school acts with integrity when it comes to the scheduling of meetings, and a compassionate run through the school calendar means that there are very few, if any, bottlenecks where staff have data deadlines and multiple meetings.

The ambitious goals of the school feature in *every* meeting. They are regularly articulated, and staff are encouraged to discuss these. There is a resilience about how people talk about the challenges they face. They are not expected to keep quiet about problems but rather to talk about them openly and honestly.

The underlying feeling is that any obstacle can be overcome, but there is sincere compassion and kindness as well as a willingness to help any member of the staff body who is suffering or not managing.

*

There are so many ways in which the values of a school can become lived through the school. The commitment to living the values has the potential to drastically alter the culture of a school, as it affects the behaviours and attitudes of all members of the community.

Some educators view a focus on these cultural aspects as 'fluffy', but I argue that they are fundamental. A commitment to 'the way we do things around here' means that eventually those behaviours and attitudes that arise out of living your values become second nature. Not having to think constantly about how one should behave and not having to consider for too long what the right course of action might need to be in a given situation frees up precious time that can be spent on the business of learning.

Relief from the stress of a valueless community is invaluable. It needs leadership, it needs adults to step up and be prepared to model the values through consistent action and reliable attitudes, and it needs a degree of faith that this work will eventually become integrated.

Key questions to help you light the way

1. How effectively are you teaching values to young people?
2. How fluent are your students in the language of values?
3. How involved are staff and students in the shaping of your school values?
4. How are the values of your school brought to life every day?
5. Are your school values living and breathing through every aspect of school life?
6. How can we ensure that all school leaders prioritise values in their work? How can you light the way towards this?

11 Confronting difficult behaviour

Chapter overview

This chapter sets out the steps we can take towards improving behaviour in our schools. It explores the difficulties that challenging student behaviour presents for staff. It considers schools' attitudes towards developing good relationships between staff and students, arguing that this should be a priority. Finally, it offers some practical support that leaders can provide their teachers with in managing behaviour. Why? Because to light the way in challenging times we must cultivate a confidence in supporting the behaviours and attitudes of young people, borne of compassion and unconditional positive regard.

We cannot escape the fact that poor behaviour in schools is a dominant topic and a huge source of anxiety. In Tom Bennett's (2017) 'Creating a culture: How school leaders can optimise behaviour', he draws attention to several sources of evidence that suggest there is a problem. On the one hand, Bennett acknowledges the 'Teacher voice omnibus' surveys from 2013 through to 2016, which suggest teachers' views on behaviour in schools have remained stable. These surveys indicate that around 76 per cent of teachers believe that behaviour in their schools is 'good' or 'better'. However, he also refers to the Ofsted 'Below the radar' report of 2014, which found that 'teachers, parents and carers are rightly concerned about the frequent loss of learning time through low-level but persistent disruptive behaviour'.

Stories of teachers leaving the profession as a consequence of the stress caused by managing poor behaviour in schools are regular features in the press. A *Guardian* report in December 2018 found that 'Three-quarters of teachers frequently have to deal with disruptive behaviour in school, and many have considered quitting as a result.' (Press Association, 2018) Similarly, a February 2019 Teacher Tapp survey found that 'Behaviour is an issue in around 30% of lessons – primary or secondary. It is particularly problematic for new teachers and contributes to them worrying about future lessons. Inconsistently applied behaviour policies increase dread and correlate with a poor Ofsted grading.' (Teacher Tapp, 2019)

The urgent nature of the issue has led to the continued playing out of arguments over which approaches to managing behaviour in schools are most effective. One cannot escape the debates over what are described as 'traditionalist' and 'progressive' approaches to behaviour management. I'm convinced that there are no benefits in trying to polarise the discussions about behaviour along progressive and traditional lines. There is so much that is shared in the foundations of how we approach managing behaviour, and it seems to me to remain the case that the problematic nature of managing behaviour comes in trying to ensure the consistency and commitment of those responsible for the system.

Thus, wherever you stand on traditional versus progressive approaches to schooling, the importance of creating an understanding of the clarity of expectation of students and staff cannot be understated. This underpins what all members of the school community understand about the culture of the school or 'the way we do things around here'.

Clarity of expectation

Rules and routines, expectations of conduct and structures provide the map for navigating the culture of an organisation. This means that the rules of your school need to match your school culture and need to enable the culture that you say you are striving for.

In my experience of special schools and pupil referral settings, the rules and structures help children in the most supportive of ways. Clarity about these rules and seeing them lived out by all members of the school community provide the security that what is said is acted upon. However, the key to getting this right is to ensure that there is genuine buy-in from all members of the school community and that the rules are not just a set of dictates created in a vacuum.

To this end, the cultural expectations should be reflective of the values of the school and should be explainable in that light. Children, staff and parents should all be able to understand why an expectation is in place, and it should be clear to them, when this expectation has not been met, that there needs to be some kind of acknowledgement of this through an appropriate sanction.

While a school should not aim to cover every potential rule there could ever be or list every kind of expected behaviour, I do think it is helpful to explore whether or not the broader expectation that, for example, 'All students treat every member of the school community with respect' is something that has been taught to young people, is constantly reinforced, is modelled by adult behaviour and is picked up upon whenever it is breached.

How are sanctions and rewards managed?

The word 'sanction' is a negatively loaded one. It is a penalty for disobedience. Instead I much prefer using 'consequences' in the context of managing behaviour. I find the term less threatening and more focused on developing the intrinsic motivation to choose well, with an understanding of how your choices will be met and what effect each choice has for yourself and others.

Passing this off as semantics is dangerous, especially in a school in which the culture you are trying to create encompasses the development of student motivation, adult empowerment, student leadership and autonomy. 'This is the punishment for breaking this rule' might elicit a different response to 'This is the consequence of not following the rule'. The latter opens up the impact of breaking rules beyond the person who has broken them and enables reflection on the numerous consequences that there are likely to be of making that choice.

Talking about following through on the consequences of not meeting behaviour expectations, as opposed to issuing sanctions, puts the teacher in a role that could, for some children, de-escalate the course of the conversation.

Having a teacher fail to explain or link a behaviour with a sanction is the cause of much classroom angst and much parent frustration. If a teacher issues a 'Warning 1', and an explanation for the reasons why is not shared, things tend to deteriorate. A reminder that the consequence for continued talking is a 'Warning 1' prepares the ground. Then explaining, 'You carried on talking so the consequence is now that you have a "Warning 1"', places the responsibility for this state of affairs squarely within the zone of control of the young person.

Relationships between teachers and students

If structures and rules provide the map of school culture, then relationships give the texture and colour of the landscape. Indeed, good relationships are the key to everything. By 'good', I do not necessarily mean that young people will always feel they like the actions of their teachers, or that teachers will always feel they like the behaviour of their students. However, good relationships are underpinned by unconditional positive regard for the other human in the situation.

For teachers, this will usually mean being prepared to do what is right for a child no matter how tough the decision may be. For students, this may mean recognising that decisions made by the adults are likely to be determined by the care and concern the teacher has for them and the desire they have to see them be successful.

When it comes to behaviour management, the teacher is positioned in the dominant role, which can, at worst, also be oppositional. But it need not be that way. Indeed, in the research carried out by the Education Endowment Foundation (2019) for their guidance on improving behaviour, there was 'a strong evidence base that teacher–pupil relationships are key to good pupil behaviour and that these relationships can affect pupil effort and academic attainment.'

Research carried out by the Violence Research Centre at Cambridge's Institute of Criminology and published in 2016 had similar insights. Here researchers found that 'students with a more positive relationship with their teacher displayed towards peers, on average, 18% more prosocial behaviour (and 10% more up to two years later), and up to 38% less aggressive behaviour (and 9% less up to four years later), over students who felt ambivalent or negative toward their teacher' (Obsuth et al., 2017).

The importance of teacher–student relationships is also made clear in the research of Joanne Golann (2015). She spent 15 months in a 'No Excuses' Charter School in a north-eastern city in the USA conducting an ethnographic study. No Excuses Charter Schools place a high value on the acquisition of reading and maths achievement, and they enforce extremely high behaviour standards through a rigorously implemented behaviour policy. What she observed was that, while school leaders wanted their students to be able to go to college and be active in their communities and society, they ended up rewarding compliance and deference at the expense of some of the skills they would need to get them into college. Golann argues in her research that 'super strictness and micromanagement […] can help schools establish order, a prerequisite for learning, but at the same time, extreme levels of control have negative consequences'. She continues that she saw many students pushing back against the strict controls and others failing to attend, so anxious were they about the culture.

The importance of good student–teacher relationships goes both ways. In a study conducted in 2012, researchers found that, for teachers, higher levels of engagement and positive emotions were present when they felt relatedness with students (Klassen et al., 2012). Indeed, relatedness with students in this study was a more important factor than relatedness with colleagues.

Yet, for some teachers, there is still antipathy towards the idea that good student relationships could be a supportive underpinning to behaviour management. In a study published in 2019, the researchers found that the centrality of good teacher–student relationships was not unambiguous and that engaging in the efforts of forming positive relationships was very much down to the individual teacher (García-Moya et al., 2019). When we look at the issues that most schools have in ensuring consistency and clarity around managing behaviour, this is clearly a problematic factor. Furthermore, the study revealed that, for some teachers, there was a perception that their authority was compromised (rather than enhanced) by their relationships with young people. Thus, the teachers who took part in the study 'seemed to be influenced by an unchallenged premise that feelings of reduced control are the consequence of too much closeness in relationships with students'. These teachers were careful to ensure, before letting their guard down, that the group of students was now 'a behaviourally safe group' and otherwise opted for a more 'controlling role' when it came to managing behaviour incidents.

How can you lead staff towards effective relationships with students?

Almost every teacher who talks about their teacher training will mention the scant amount of training that was made available to them for managing behaviour. Yet, evidence of the importance of developing cooperative relationships with students is compelling. It, therefore, falls to us as leaders to ensure that adequate time and space are created to develop teachers' interpersonal skills and their ability to form healthy and productive relationships with young people.

Get the balance right

Having good relationships with students does not mean that everything goes their way. Encourage adults in your school to reflect on their confidence with being assertive. This should be bread and butter to most teachers, but some teachers will need instruction, and you can help them in the following ways:

1. Coach them in authoritative speech and actions, and model for them the way that voice and body language have a bearing on student responses.

2. Encourage them to be upstanding – at the door at transitions and around and about the classroom (rather than desk-bound) during lessons.

3. Teach them the PEP approach of using proximity and maintaining and using eye contact, as well as privacy, instead of launching into a telling off. Thus, teachers are encouraged to move in more closely to a student (proximity), make sure they have been seen (eye contact), and then discreetly affirm the desired behaviours (privacy).

Find out about your students

Knowing students' names and being aware of what is going on in their lives sounds obvious, but I've known teachers who were having persistent difficulties with students who undermined their efforts to turn things around by continually getting the students' names wrong. Make sure that your staff invest time in finding out about students. Ensuring that your team members prioritise this most basic of human interactions will pay dividends.

Catch them doing great things

If staff members in your school routinely notice and comment on students getting things right, it will really help them in their efforts to develop cooperative relationships with students. It will also reinforce the cultural expectations of the school.

Set standards for discourse with staff

Most staff don't need to be supported in this area, but I have met staff who have struggled to recognise that the way they were communicating was not fostering a positive relationship. For these staff members, being able to reflect unconditional positive regard for students sets them on a steep learning curve.

Conversations that support and develop team members in this area need to be sensitively, not judgementally, handled. Staff need to be given space to see the detrimental effects their views on the power dynamics between them and their charges have – how they influence their language and, in turn, impact on their relationships.

Don't worry – it's not a zero-sum game

Some teachers argue that the students who play up get all the attention and that this has a negative impact on other students who are typically well behaved. I was well behaved at school, and I did well even though my teachers focused a lot of their time and attention on managing the behaviour of other students in the class. The thing is that I didn't mind one bit. I could see (as most kids can) that someone else really needed the attention that I was lucky enough to get at home. I could see that someone else struggled in ways I didn't, and I was glad that my teachers were there to help.

The problem with the zero-sum game, as it applies to the classroom, is that it suggests that the attention of the teacher on a group of needy students somehow means everyone else loses. A rather more abundant depiction of the scenario might have it that other classmates learn independence, autonomy, about the luck of their circumstances and about the advantages of helping others in society. When we worry that our actions disproportionally favour one group, we are in danger of missing the point.

Use positive classroom behaviours for all

That being said, as the educational researcher Robert Marzano (2003) points out in his research into the effectiveness of behaviour management approaches, there are subtle ways in which teachers can communicate their interest in all students that definitely do not detract from the majority but in fact enhance cooperation in the room. Marzano suggests that teachers can:

1. Make eye contact with each student, being sure to scan the room and get coverage of the entire space.
2. Deliberately gain closer proximity with each student over the course of the lesson.
3. Make sure that all students are recognised for bringing their ideas and call out their contributions. So, for example, 'Shazia just built on Rohan's point really effectively.'
4. Encourage all students to participate in class discussion.
5. Give plenty of wait time to allow for processing and to enable all students the chance to give feedback.

In another of his books, *Classroom Management That Works* (Marzano et al., 2003), Marzano talks about the importance of 'mental set' when it comes to classroom management. Mental set is a kind of mindfulness applied to the classroom context and is unpacked into two areas: 'withitness' and 'emotional objectivity'.

Withitness

When explaining 'withitness', Marzano points to Jacob Kounin, another educational theorist, who coined the term. A teacher with withitness will be able to act on potential problems and anticipate behaviour issues quickly. Withitness is achieved by the constant awareness of what is happening in the classroom, whether you are talking one on one with a student or supporting a small group; the rest of the class does not go unnoticed.

Withitness strategies include the below, and these can be shared with all staff to supplement their behaviour management toolkit:

- Be alert to the hot spots in your classroom and have a plan for cooling them down.
- Scan the class regularly and make eye contact with as many of your students as you can.
- Always intervene promptly. Don't let issues run and run but make sure that your pupils know straight away what the consequences of disruptive behaviour will be.
- Use the PEP approach, as mentioned on page 134.
- Use plenty of non-verbal cues to encourage good learning behaviours. These can seem quite obvious but signalling silence by putting your finger to your lips is tried and true!

Emotional objectivity

Emotional objectivity is an aspect of mental set that I think has the potential to influence cooperative and productive relationships with students significantly.

Emotional objectivity is the ability to see behaviour as a set of circumstances without attaching negative thought to the behaviour or the way in which the child deals with the consequences of their poor choices. Far from removing the personal connection with young people, emotional objectivity does not come from feeling less about the child; indeed, it arises out of positive regard that does not personalise the behaviour of the child. Teachers who can display emotional objectivity are not hurt or angered by poor behaviour and can regulate their own emotions to meet this state of objectivity for the benefit of the child. As I have said on countless occasions, 'you cannot manage what *you* cannot manage'. Thus, for staff who struggle to regulate their own behaviour, behaviour management is likely to be tricky, draining and unproductive.

But there are ways that you can help as a leader. If you find that a teacher is having particular difficulty with the behaviour of a group or individual and that this is escalating, it is worth considering supporting them to look at the child through the lens of emotional objectivity.

This enables you to support the teacher in all of the usual ways – implementing the behaviour policy and ensuring that consequences are correctly implemented – but it also allows you the chance to alter the course of the teacher's emotional reality and move them from distress, stress or anxiety to a more confident sense of self. It is a simple coaching exercise and best undertaken when tempers are not too inflamed and when emotions are closer.

Developing emotional objectivity
Ask the teacher to:

1. Describe the current situation in detail, sticking only to facts and not to the interpretation of the facts. Thus, the teacher can describe: 'Robert in Year 10 interrupted me while I was speaking and spoke to another child when I had asked for silence' or 'Robert in Year 10 overturned a desk and hit another pupil with a rolled-up exercise book'. What they must not do at this point is colour in their description of the facts with their interpretations, as these are likely to be negative. So, the teacher must be encouraged to reframe statements like 'Robert in Year 10 totally undermined me with his continual disruptive behaviour while I was trying to teach' or 'Robert trashed the classroom, overturning tables and chairs'. They must stick to facts that could be verified and are not open to interpretation.

2. After this, ask the teacher to describe the thoughts they have concerning the facts they have described. This is the time for 'Robert totally undermined my authority' or 'The classroom environment was made unsafe' and so forth.

3. When this is done, ask the teacher to go back to the facts and see whether they can find a set of more neutral thoughts they could choose to have to replace the ones they have expressed. The reason this is important is that a different set of conscious thoughts will influence the teacher's ability to gain emotional objectivity. Thus, 'Robert must have been incredibly angry about something to overturn the table' or 'For some reason, Robert wanted my attention or to gain the attention of his peers' can provide more helpful emotions.

4. Notice that these thoughts don't excuse Robert's behaviour and they don't mean that there will be no consequences for Robert's actions, but they do mean that the behaviour is depersonalised, and that enquiry and curiosity rather than hostility can prevail.

Teaching positive behaviour

When I made the transition from mainstream schools into PRUs and special schools, I remember being struck by the fact that, because there was an expectation that many of the young people would struggle to manage their behaviour, the institutions prepared themselves for it and set out to teach positive behaviour as part of the curriculum offer. I had been in schools in which the response to challenging behaviour was mainly in reaction to what had occurred, and I had never considered the potential for teaching behaviour to students.

At best, we can assume that students come to most educational settings having been taught how to behave either at home, in nursery or in primary school. However, unlike with maths and English, where we assume that ongoing instruction is required to match the maturation of the brain and the development of the human, our behaviour instruction in schools often falls short.

In PRUs and many special schools, the emphasis on teaching social skills is present. We introduced family dining in our school, and in all the pupil referral settings I have managed, there was particular importance placed on adults spending time with students during lunches and breaktimes. In these times, the staff would model productive and positive conversations and relationships, they would make snacks for and with young people, and they would encourage students in communication that foregrounded turn-taking, listening and table manners. Staff also facilitated play on the courts and in the playgrounds during social time to model communication, collaboration and dealing with challenging situations. These situations fostered good relationships between staff and students but were also essential teaching time.

Restorative practices

When The Teachers' Union (NASUWT) claimed that restorative practices were leading to teacher blaming (NASUWT, 2019), several teachers echoed their agreement across social media. I agree that restorative practices are not the be-all and end-all of a behaviour system, but I do think they can be usefully integrated into an array of consequences that every behaviour system will have.

In special schools and PRUs, restorative practices can provide a framework for teaching students who do not know how to handle and manage conflict tools they can use for the rest of their lives.

A restorative circle is a great tool to build community and it can then be used to support restorative discussions. If you want to establish the use of restorative circles in your classroom or school, there are a host of resources online and organisations that can support you. What is important is that the routine of working restoratively, of sitting in circles and communicating in this way, have been established before you attempt to deal with weighty issues using this method.

Restorative circles start as community building and they establish the psychological safety that will later be required if and when the group need to confront challenging issues. These community-building circles give students the chance to get to know each other better and they allow students to talk about non-controversial subjects. They also establish the rules of engagement, can be fun and are a basis for sharing.

- Restorative circles always begin with a stated purpose and a reminder (or teaching) of the circle guidelines.
- Next there is a check-in with each member of the circle to establish connectedness.
- The community-building activity is next (or, if you are well practised at circles, an activity that addresses a particular issue can be brought to the circle).
- The next phase is a check-out round.
- Finally, the circle is closed and participants are thanked for their contributions.

When used well, restorative circles give students a set of language and tools to discuss things that have gone wrong. When used badly, they attempt to tackle issues that are too serious for the psychological maturity of the teacher or group and issues are not satisfactorily dealt with. Thus, teachers need to be judicious about the kinds of issues that are brought to restorative circles, and I am not advocating for each and every incident, no matter the seriousness, to be put through the framework of a restorative circle. However, using them on a daily basis to consider low-level issues that may be affecting the climate of the classroom creates consistency and begins to create the schema for young people to build upon.

*

This chapter has explored some of the ways schools and leaders can respond to difficult behaviours when they present themselves in school. It has set out the importance of establishing positive teacher–student relationships as they impact well on both staff and young people. It has also explored a range of strategies that leaders can develop with teachers in order to build their confidence in managing difficult behaviour. Finally, it has considered the use of restorative practices as one additional intervention that can be used by leaders wanting to manage difficult behaviour as well as build strong school communities.

Key questions to help you light the way

1. How clear are the expectations of conduct in your school?
2. How are sanctions discussed and framed for young people?
3. How positive would students be about student–staff relationships?
4. How supportive is the leadership of staff who are struggling with managing behaviour?
5. How could you use the strategies outlined in this chapter to support colleagues who are struggling with managing behaviour?
6. How effectively does your school teach children how to behave?
7. How can we ensure that every child in every school is supported by adults who offer them unconditional positive regard? How can you light the way towards this?

12 School exclusions

Chapter overview

This chapter sets out how to manage the challenge of school exclusions as an ethical leader. It explores some of the reasons why exclusion rates are not falling fast enough. It considers the impact that funding levels have had on school exclusions, before then offering advice on how to proceed ethically and correctly should you need to exclude a child. Why? Because to light the way in challenging times, leaders, regardless of the actions of others, must uphold their commitment to fair, honest and ethical action.

In Chapter 10, page 120, we looked at how leaders can go about creating a values-based culture in their school, and in the last chapter we explored solutions to supporting positive behaviour. In this chapter, we are moving on to look at what happens when children don't want to behave in accordance with the school's values. Throughout my career, I have been a leader who is committed to inclusion. I have worked in schools in challenging circumstances in which many, many children could have been excluded but I have argued strongly that they be given a further chance to stay. This chapter is about managing exclusions and maintaining an inclusionary outlook.

School exclusions: the current state

The Timpson Review (Timpson, 2019) provides an important recent starting point to gain a perspective on the state of school exclusions in 2019. Although the review points out that exclusions have not reached the high point of 2006, when comparative records began, they have been climbing since 2013. The Timpson Review argues that discussions about school behaviour tend to be rather unhelpfully polarised, with one side believing that poor behaviour is either a choice or comes as a result of a lack of boundaries and, at the other end of the spectrum, some teachers and leaders arguing that challenging behaviour is the communication of unmet needs.

Whatever the cause of challenging behaviour in schools, according to a report by the Policy Exchange (Williams, 2018), the impact of trying to manage challenging behaviour sees nearly two-thirds of teachers considering leaving the profession. Furthermore, almost three-quarters of teachers polled agreed that teachers were being put off from joining the profession for fear of becoming victim to poor behaviour. Indeed, in 2016–17, 745 permanent exclusions and 26,695 fixed-term exclusions came as a consequence of the physical assault of an adult (Timpson, 2019).

As a school leader, I have seen the effects on staff, including the stress and the anxiety caused by the feeling that they cannot manage student behaviour. I have seen young and new teachers leave the profession as a consequence, but I have also seen the impact of exclusion on children and families.

The impact of exclusion

Data cited in the Timpson Review tells us that, in 2015–16, just seven per cent of children who were permanently excluded and 18 per cent of children who received multiple mixed-period exclusions achieved good passes in English and maths. And this is just the beginning of the story for these children. The impact of exclusion has many other devastating and far-reaching effects.

According to the 2017 report 'Making the difference' by the Institute for Public Policy (Gill et al., 2017), only one per cent of excluded young people gain five good GCSEs including English and maths. We might say that lots of children don't manage to achieve a set of results that allows them successful entry into the world of work aged 16, but the report highlights the stark difference in outcomes for young people who are excluded by the time they reach 20. For young people who have not been excluded from school, the majority of them (87 per cent) gain a Level 2 qualification by the time they are 20. For children who have been excluded, only 30 per cent achieve this level of qualification by the same age.

According to the HM Chief Inspector for England and Wales Annual Report of 2014–15 (HM Inspectorate of Prisons, 2015), a survey conducted with young men in custody revealed that 'Eighty-five per cent of boys reported that they had been excluded from school before they came into detention, 73% said they had truanted from school at some time, and 41% were 14 or younger when they last attended school.' This is backed up by Gill et al. (2017), who point out that 'a longitudinal study of prisoners [published by the Ministry of Justice in 2012] found that 63 per cent of prisoners reported being temporarily excluded when at school [...] Forty-two per cent had been permanently excluded, and these excluded prisoners were more likely to be repeat offenders than other prisoners.'

Timpson argues that it would be wrong to suggest that exclusion causes young people to commit crime or that preventing exclusion would in itself prevent crime. However, a cross-party group of MPs and peers investigating knife crime are concerned that exclusions can be a potent trigger for young people who end up committing knife crime. They draw a correlation between knife crime and exclusion in their report 'Back to school? Breaking the link between school exclusions and knife crime' (All-Party Parliamentary Group on Knife Crime, 2019).

Progress 8

Ranking schools according to the Progress 8 measure is problematic for many settings that have high numbers of vulnerable children. The consequence of this measure and of the expectation that a particular set of subjects will be applicable to meet the needs and interests and thus secure the engagement of every child has, for many settings, been extremely challenging.

The facts are that many disadvantaged students don't fare well in the Progress 8 measure. Indeed, a parliamentary committee convened in 2018 found that disadvantaged children are being 'disproportionately excluded', in part as an 'unintended and unfortunate consequence' of the government's focus on progress measures (House of Commons Education Committee, 2018). And the facts are also that schools don't fare well when they don't meet the expected Progress 8 measure. It has a negative impact on their reputation and on school intake numbers, which will inevitably lead to challenges with funding. Researchers at the University of Exeter found that, in fact, '40 per cent of "underperforming" secondary schools would no longer fall into the category if progress measures were re-weighted to account for pupils' backgrounds' (Staufenberg, 2019).

What this means is that certain groups of students are being punished and certain schools are too. With leaders often unable to meet the needs and interests of students and with the awareness that their funding, future and reputation cannot withstand the pressures of an unsatisfactory Progress 8 score, a context is created around exclusions that means it is almost impossible for certain young people to succeed. Timpson (2019) refers to 'exclusion in all but name' in his report, and the rise in off-rolling (the practice of taking students off the school roll without formally excluding them) seems to correlate strongly with the pressure for schools to achieve the Progress 8 measure. In September 2019, Ofsted published a blog (Bradbury, 2019) in which it is suggested that the number of schools suspected of off-rolling had risen by 13 per cent in one year.

Funding

Funding too has a significant part to play in the decisions that school leaders are making when it comes to exclusions. The Timpson Review reveals that 78 per cent of permanent exclusions issued in 2016–17 were to pupils with SEND or who were classified as in need. These are alarming statistics, but they bear out my experience in that many schools have been struggling since the 2014 SEND funding reforms, which saw the introduction of education, health and care plans (EHCPs) but a lack of funding to match the continued levels of need.

I have had the fortune to work on both sides of the provision divide. I have been a senior leader in charge of inclusion in a mainstream school and a senior leader in a SEMH school. I have also been a headteacher within the pupil referral service and a headteacher in a large mainstream comprehensive with a significant provision for students with SEND.

I can attest to the difference that having increased funding levels made in the early 2000s in an inner-city mainstream school. It gave us the ability to create a genuinely inclusive environment that met the needs of the majority of students.

We had a large resource base, and we were able to set up alternative provision in-house. There was a fully functioning local inclusion managers group in which managed moves were handled. There were staff available to support managed moves and to address issues as they arose. This significantly reduced the likelihood of a managed move failing. Exclusions did occur, but they were rare in my school, I would say because we typically had the funding to undertake a lot of preventative work and, because of this, the excessive burden of disruption was taken out of the classroom. There was a feeling that there were many routes to try out before exclusion needed to occur.

I can also attest to the luxury of working in a SEMH special school in which every child had an appropriately funded EHCP. For these children and their families, there was a relief and a reassurance that their children's needs could be met and the endless merry-go-round of fixed-term exclusion, falling behind, bad news from the school and the threat of permanent exclusion had come to an end. It was astonishing for me to go from a relatively well-funded mainstream setting and see the difference that a fully funded special school place could make to a child's life.

I can attest, two years later, to the experience of leading an education-other-than-at-school service in a local authority in which certain schools had become reliant on the funding levels that had supported the PRUs and sixth-day provision unit. My first experiences were so disappointing. I found many children who had been failed by the systems that should have worked for them. Rather than children being appropriately assessed and thus getting the places they needed in a special school, many had been excluded into a pupil referral system that meant no cost or responsibility lay with the schools anymore. The sixth-day provision was almost always full and, to my dismay, it was often used by schools as a means of giving the rest of the school community a breather. The correlation between regular visits to the sixth-day provision and permanent exclusion was strong, and it was not long before our frequent attendees found their way to the Key Stage 3 or 4 PRU. The funding levels over the years had made certain schools lazy. Funding had encouraged a lack of inclusionary practice, and this travesty meant that best use was not always being made of the money. There were some excellent schools and some excellent practice and, in my experience, these were the schools that, when it came to it, were able to cope when the funding levels dropped. These were the schools that had systems and structures to support all learners and had, and continued to have, very low exclusion rates.

More recently, back in the context of a mainstream school, and this time as headteacher, I have faced the conflicting and, at times, confusing emotions one has about exclusions from school. I cannot fathom why more is not made of the relationship between a child's vulnerability in school and the presence of poverty, poor mental or physical health, drugs and alcohol, and so forth. As more and more children are plunged into poverty, I cannot understand why the headlines are not rich with the injustice of cuts to school funding. And why there is not more acknowledgement that the true cost will be higher levels of social exclusion is beyond me.

A nuanced decision

Whatever goes into a headteacher's decision to exclude, it is a nuanced decision and it is so unhelpful to have the polarisation of views paraded about Twitter as though if you tend toward one ideology you will naturally behave in one way – all of the time.

Most schools scaffold the child, the family and the school's understanding of how a child is able or unable to manage their behaviour through some sort of tiered system. Certainly, in the schools I have worked in, children would move through various stages of support and intervention. The hope would always be that, with the right support, they would work their way back down through the tiers but, for many children, this isn't the case.

My experience has been in local authorities that have agreements between secondary schools around managed moves. These agreements mean that, if a child looks to be reaching the final stages of the middle tier of intervention, the school might suggest that a managed move be considered to an alternative school. This is not a forced move, but a move taken under consideration by all parties if it seems it would support a fresh start.

Managed moves, because they are voluntary, can be successful. When I was an inclusion lead in the mid-2000s, managed moves were supported by a number of members of staff, and a small team would meet with the child and their family on a regular basis to review the progress of the move and to celebrate positives. This focus on a new start made a huge difference, as did the presence of a member of staff from the child's previous school, which was a positive indicator that they had not been abandoned but that everybody wanted to see them being successful.

As headteacher of the pupil referral service, my staff were fundamental to the smooth running of the managed move process. One member of my team knew all the schools in the local authority so well that he was able to support the discussions about which school might work best for a young person. Members of our behaviour support team were able to accompany the child into their new school for a few sessions after the move. They would then run mentoring sessions with the child to build their resilience for the brave step they had taken in trying a fresh start in a new school. This was all supported by regular meetings at which all parties – the previous school, present school, behaviour support team mentor and the family – were present.

However, without the resources to coordinate smooth and intentional processes around managed moves, children who have arrived mid-year or midway through their school career now often find the transition very problematic. While transition meetings do take place, they are often one-off events and they lack the follow-up and infrastructure of a small team around the child that is needed. The feeling of abandonment by their previous school is palpable, but the prior school is not always at fault here; they simply may not have the ability to get out of school to attend a supportive transition meeting.

I've met children who had reached the stage of a managed move just two terms into arriving at secondary school. I've met many children whose parents have moved them to a new secondary school, for fear they were about to be pushed, only to find that six weeks on their child is placed on a managed move to yet another school.

The tragedy for these children is that no one takes responsibility for them. The services that used to exist to hold the process also synthesised vital information about the child into transfer documents that would enable future schools to build on and act on all the support and intervention that had previously been put in place.

What I have found more and more is that information sharing is hampered by frazzled staff not passing on details in a timely fashion, by the lack of capacity to properly support managed moves for these children and by the fact that so many families are jumping before being pushed. This means that, in effect, they are cutting out any of the formal mechanisms that schools use when they admit a vulnerable child onto their roll.

A tangled web

A factor that unites the young people that I describe as being unable to thrive in mainstream settings is that they have often been boys. As a headteacher in the pupil referral service and as a senior leader in a special SEMH school, the gender imbalance was staggering. Recent research by The Centre for Education and Youth (Millard et al., 2018) shows us that black Caribbean and white free-school-meal-eligible boys are part of cohorts that typically underachieve, and this was frequently born out in my experience in schools.

Again, this is where I find that we enter into unhelpful polarisations of the issues. The nuances about the decision to exclude or not come when one looks at the experiences of bias and injustice certain children face just as part of their day-to-day school life. I have seen black boys whose behaviours have resembled the behaviours of other children be perceived to be more threatening by certain teachers. I have heard unqualified statements about the likelihood of a black boy (who was very tall) potentially doing something in school that might lead to serious injury. This member of staff wanted him excluded just in case. I refused.

Many schools will say they look beyond race and they look beyond class, but they don't, and rooting out the terrible injustice faced by some members of our communities is a critical role that the headteacher must fulfil. Where I have refused to exclude, it often comes as a consequence of hearing what a child has had to endure within a system in which the odds are stacked against them.

Sometimes a child will say a teacher has it in for them and is not treating them fairly. When headteachers know that there is unconscious bias at the heart of the desire to see a child excluded from the community, they should not exclude. That being said, a child will often sense the collective hostility and will know when there is no will for them succeed, so often their behaviour accelerates beyond the point of salvation.

No one ever wants to be PEXed

One of the things you never want to do as a headteacher is to permanently exclude (PEX) a child. I challenge any teacher who is happy to tweet about how many more children should be permanently excluded to make it through a PEX meeting untouched.

A common thread with the children I am talking about is that none of them wanted to be excluded. No matter what they have done and no matter how badly they may have messed up, no child I have ever met in a PEX meeting wanted to leave the school.

When you take the decision to permanently exclude a child, you take the decision to contribute towards a long line of social exclusions, and this is why everything a leader does in the run up to it, everything that takes place within the process and everything that happens afterwards must signal to the child that there is a way back for them (although not back to your school) and that all is not lost.

If you do need to take the decision to permanently exclude a child, there are things you can do to make sure the process is right and fair and leaves everyone with their dignity intact. The following makes some suggestions as to how.

Fair and ethical management of the exclusion process

First of all, get the 'them vs us' mentality out of your head. As a headteacher, it is vital that you know exactly what proper exclusion practice is and that you ensure that you have shared as much information as possible with the parents. You want to be in a meeting in which all 'Is' have been dotted and all 'Ts' crossed because that means that you and your school have done everything within your power to prevent this exclusion. Many experienced leaders will already have a strong grasp of this process, but I hope this section is helpful for new leaders who are not yet clear on what good practice looks like.

The School Exclusion Project (2019) sets out a number of helpful points of guidance for leaders who are facing excluding pupils. I share these below as a framework for helping you to develop your own best practice guidance.

When should permanent exclusion take place?

Permanent exclusion should only take place when there has been a serious breach of the school's behaviour policy.

The assumption that the behaviour policy has been well executed must be checked. 'Persistent disruptive behaviour' is the most enduring and common reason for both permanent and fixed-term exclusions. School leaders must be confident that the persistence of this disruptive behaviour could not have been pre-empted or managed differently.

The Framework for Ethical Leadership (Ethical Leadership Commission, 2019) gives a helpful reminder here: headteachers should be just – acting fairly and working for the good of all children – and they should be wise – using their experience and insight to check that persistent disruptive behaviour is being monitored and that interventions are having impact. Their honesty and openness along the journey should mean that, if and when the decision needs to be taken to permanently exclude a child on these grounds, the child and their family are in no doubt that the school has tried everything in its power to do the right thing.

Exclusions must follow the most up-to-date guidance

The current guidance for England (Department for Education, 2017) and Scotland (Scottish Government, 2017) is from 2017. Welsh guidance (Welsh Government, 2019) was updated in 2019 and guidance for Northern Ireland is from 1998 (Department of Education). These documents are ones that all members of the SLT should have a clear understanding of. Their work contributes towards ensuring that any exclusion that takes place in school is done with ethical consideration and that every step towards a possible exclusion is conducted in a manner that reflects the values of the school.

I have found that many staff, including many senior leaders, have a patchy understanding of exclusions. It is an area that is typically left to the pastoral deputy head, and as such can be a real vulnerability for new headteachers who have had their backgrounds in curriculum, teaching and learning or raising achievement.

For this reason, I urge SLTs to put exclusions guidance on their agenda and run it through the lens of their values. Ensure that they are clear about what kinds of messages, what tone and what register they will want to be using if they reach the point at which exclusion is necessary. Permanent exclusion should be sobering. It should be something that the school community takes seriously and understands. The legal context and the significant social ramifications of exclusion can bring this home to colleagues, which is why I highly recommend having the facts about permanent exclusion and the Department for Education exclusion guidance tabled at a full-staff meeting.

Exclusions must be officially recorded as exclusions

There is no code for 'cooling off'. The exclusion code must be used for the half day or full day that exclusion has taken place.

Exclusions must be for disciplinary reasons only

Schools cannot exclude students because they don't attend or because they are unlikely to succeed at the end of a key stage. Likewise, illness and poor mental health are not grounds for exclusions.

All schools must have a behaviour policy for pupils to follow

If it looks as though a child is spiralling up the stages of the behaviour policy towards exclusion, leaders should check for a full understanding of the behaviour policy and its consequences.

They should also ensure that all support and sanctions are properly reviewed for the impact they are having. If there is no impact as a result of interventions, has the school changed tack and tried something different? The school should be very clear on what the patterns are with regard to children demonstrating persistent disruptive behaviour and should understand and seek to be clear on the underlying reasons for it.

Headteachers should, as far as possible, avoid permanently excluding looked-after children

Data published in 2018 on how well looked-after children fare in UK schools had some heartening news. The collective responsibility the sector has taken to ensure that looked-after children are not permanently excluded has seen this figure drop to its lowest in five years (Ward, 2018). That said, looked-after children were five times more likely to be temporarily excluded than pupils overall. For a cohort of children for whom stability is absolutely critical, these figures are still unacceptably high. To mitigate this, schools should consider all the reasonable adjustments that can be made for this cohort of children.

Headteachers should also, as far as possible, avoid excluding children with EHCPs

According to 2016–17 data, children with SEND are six times more likely to be excluded than other children: 'Pupils with identified special educational needs (SEN) accounted for around half of all permanent exclusions (46.7 per cent) and fixed period exclusions (44.9 per cent)'. (Tirraoro, 2018) This data is already concerning but it also masks the numbers of children who have had no diagnosis of SEND. This is the reason I suggest a sustained and consistent approach to intervention that tries to address what the underlying causes of poor behaviour might be. Yes, the assessment process takes time, but it is a route we have at our disposal, and we need to hope that we can reach the end of the process before we get to the end of the road for a child in school.

Pupils cannot be excluded for poor academic attainment

Back to the Timpson Review (see page 141) to remind us that off-rolling is not an option. It isn't, but neither is making no adjustments whatsoever to provision in ways that ensure that certain children will become persistently disruptive and then be excluded. The pressures of school progress measures cannot have as their unintended consequences the decimated life chances of children.

The headteacher's decision to exclude must be taken on the 'balance of probabilities'

Integrity and objectivity come into play when a headteacher has to consider the 'balance of probabilities'. It takes courage and wisdom too. To sit and listen with an open heart and an enquiring mind to the events as they are explained by staff, students and sometimes just the one student who is at risk of exclusion, and then determine a fair outcome, is the real stuff of leadership. Headteachers should have in place a small group of people that they can talk their thinking through with to ensure that this balance has been given due consideration and that decisions are not rushed.

Headteachers must also find out whether there is anything that hasn't already been mentioned at school by other members of the school community that will help them come to the right decision. Rushing through a permanent exclusion and acting from the position of upset or anger at an event that has occurred is never a good idea.

In some cases, it may be appropriate to issue a fixed-term exclusion, pending a decision about permanent exclusion. This will give you time to gather the necessary facts and seek the relevant advice. It is remarkable how, as a head, you can be convinced, particularly when a one-off serious incident occurs, that permanent exclusion is the only answer. If you allow there to be space between ensuring you understand all of the facts of the incident and deciding on the sanction, this will help you to have the confidence that you are acting justly.

At the very least, headteachers should ask themselves:

1. Is there anything happening at school that is exacerbating the situation?

2. Has anything happened at school that could be contributing towards the situation?

3. Has anything happened outside of school that has contributed to the situation (bereavement, witnessing domestic violence and so on)?

4. Has anything happened outside of school in the past that is, for whatever reason, having a bearing on the situation now?

It is remarkable the amount of information we hold in our collective knowledge of children in our schools, and every avenue must be explored for the impact they have today on the behaviour of children in your care. This means that painstaking research into the presence of bullying, mental health issues, bereavement, unidentified SEND, presence of domestic violence and so forth should take place.

No headteacher wants to be in a permanent exclusion meeting and find that these stones have been left unturned. Indeed, if the permanent exclusion needs to take place, you want to be assured, as the headteacher, that you have understood everything about the antecedents to the exclusion and that you have done everything in your power to try to avoid it.

*

This chapter has explored the ways in which school leaders can ensure that, if they do need to take steps to exclude children, this is done with a full awareness of ethical and legal considerations. In setting out some of the ethical dilemmas that external pressures, for example Progress 8, have posed for some headteachers, it has reasserted the need to ensure that the entitlement to education for all children, and in particular vulnerable children, is met.

Key questions to help you light the way

1. Have you analysed your exclusions data and checked them for any bias?
2. Are you and your staff familiar with the legal framework around permanent exclusions?
3. Do you and your staff understand the social implications of permanent exclusions?
4. Are you and your SLT familiar with the most up-to-date guidance on exclusions?
5. Have you run your exclusion practices through the lens of your school values?
6. How can we ensure that every child, in every school, is met with fair, honest and ethical action when it comes to exclusions? How can you light the way towards this?

PART 5

Leading beyond the school

13 Breakthrough conversations with parents

Chapter overview

This chapter sets out the way in which breakthrough conversations with parents can lead everyone to a better understanding of the journey we are on. It gives leaders a framework for holding potentially challenging conversations with parents. It demonstrates through case study the success, hidden and overt, that can be found when we commit our heart and will to 'sitting in the fire' with parents. Why? Because to light the way in challenging times we need leaders who are prepared to use courage and integrity to guide and support the wider school community.

When I talk about breakthrough conversations, I am talking about a conversation with a parent that is transformative and in which both parties find themselves entering a new phase in their relationship.

Most conversations leave people in a different state afterwards than they were in before. However, a breakthrough conversation with a parent can be one that enables all future discussions to begin with the utter confidence that you, as a professional, genuinely have the best interests of the child and the family at heart. The willingness to participate as a leader and as a human being brings everyone's vulnerability to the room and means that it is not just the parent who is expected to be laid bare to the painful emotions and issues that may be at play.

These conversations can happen in an unplanned situation when you are unprepared. I always recommend that if a parent wants to have an impromptu meeting, you take the opportunity to listen (if you have time) but then try to book an appropriate time and place to meet properly. It can be challenging to divert a parent when an urgent issue has arisen but, if the problems are to be taken seriously and end with serious results, then the right space needs to be created for the meeting to take place. It might be that the meeting needs to take place in an hour, or it could be the next day but, as you will see, preparation is so crucial for these meetings to go well.

Preparation is critical

Preparation for these meetings is the most important thing you can put in place. Your preparation for a breakthrough conversation with a parent will influence how much parents feel able to trust in you as a human and as a leader. There are two types of preparation needed. The first is practical and the second is mental.

Practical preparation

If you know the parent will be coming into the meeting with other young children, make sure you have a room that can accommodate their needs. Parents with newborns or toddlers will need space for buggies and prams. It can be helpful to have materials for younger children to play with to enable the adults to concentrate on the meeting.

If you are discussing an issue to do with a child who needs to be at the school while the meeting is taking place, but you don't want them to hear all of the discussion, ensure that there are other members of staff around who can support with supervision.

I mention this in the next chapter, but I will say it again: a parent who has been busy all day and has been rushing about may not have had time to have a drink or eat before the meeting. Offering a cuppa and a biscuit is not only a welcoming gesture but will also provide a vital boost to blood sugar levels, which may be needed during the meeting.

Have all the records, evidence and properly filled-in paperwork you need for the meeting. If you are going to reference class books, then have these available. Poorly marked books and behaviour records with inappropriate staff comments in them will not help your case. Provide information that will support you all in getting the results that genuinely serve the child, and that will help the parents understand the issues that you are trying to address.

Mental preparation

Mental preparation is, as far as I am concerned, as important as (if not more important than) practical preparation if you are to lead a breakthrough conversation. We can change the language about these conversations – they can be hard, and that's OK, but the way we think about hard things is the key element that we need to address.

Change your thoughts about difficult meetings

If you think to yourself that the upcoming meeting you have with Parent X is going to be trying, your feelings about the potential meeting will range from anxiety through to full-blown terror. Acting from a position of dread or terror will never create the results that I am confident you are hoping for.

So, how can you change the way you feel about these meetings?

Well, you can start by calling them 'breakthrough conversations' rather than 'difficult' ones. A breakthrough is something exciting, something to look forward to, and there is the other side of the breakthrough that has us anticipating a new world.

If you acknowledge that you need to have a breakthrough conversation with Parent X, you can, in all likelihood, experience the thought, 'I'm interested to see where this conversation gets us.' Having had the experience of success with breakthrough conversations, you might even start to relish them. Indeed, your thoughts could quite realistically become 'I enjoy working through the tensions of breakthrough conversations' or 'I learn so much in these kinds of conversations with parents, about myself and other humans.'

I have found that choosing to term 'difficult meetings' with parents as 'breakthrough conversations', I do have thoughts of 'I enjoy working through difficulty to reach resolution.' For me, this thought evokes a sense of calm. It is my ambition that all leaders and teachers experience this sense of peace when it comes to situations they have previously found challenging.

If you want to influence the tone of the meeting and you want to feel confident or calm, and if you're going to feel peaceful or composed, you need to choose thoughts that get you there. You will then find that you can use these feelings to fuel the kind of conversation you want to have but also to influence your body language, your greeting, your empathy and communication in general.

Understanding the link between the way you think and your feelings is critical. And once you know how you want to feel, you can ensure that this feeling inspires the language you choose and the entire way that you show up.

How to have a breakthrough conversation

The following sets out some step-by-step guidance to having breakthrough conversations with parents.

Set the tone

Set out the results that you would like from the meeting and offer the parents and the child the chance to think about what results they would like from the meeting too. The ownership of the meeting is not yours. This is a joint meeting, and the outcomes of the meeting should prioritise the child and incorporate the views of everyone.

A general agenda helps give the meeting structure and enables you to move on when you need to and circle back to an area that is getting stuck. The agenda that is created should arise out of the above conversation about shared outcomes.

Thus, the initial conversation in a breakthrough conversation might go something like this:

School leader: So, I have invited you in because I thought it might be helpful for us to try to problem-solve some of the things that have been happening in school. What are you hoping to resolve during this meeting?

Parent: I'd like to know why the school has been so useless at supporting my child, and I want you to stop calling me in the day as I have to keep missing work.

School leader: OK, so ideally for you, at the end of the meeting, we'll have a really clear map of the support and interventions that have been put in place, and we can look at where the gaps are. For my part, I would like to make sure you are clear on the incidents that have been occurring and what we have been doing to intervene or support. I'd also like to set out a new plan for Johnny moving forward.

Stick to the facts

The facts are neutral, and it can be helpful to say that you are going to, as much as possible, be neutral. Language can be so emotively used, and this is why it is incredibly important to check through behaviour records before you present them.

We are often told that we need to start meetings with all the positives, but I think that's a bit like when you are on a sales call, and you know you are about to get pitched, so you can't relax and listen to the information being given. Adult conversations don't need to be sandwiched with good, bad, good. Indeed, something along the lines of the following would be best:

School leader: It might be helpful for us all to be as neutral as we can and start with what's been going on for Johnny. Do you want to start by telling me what's been going on at home?

Parent: Everything's been fine. / We've been having a really hard time.

School leader: OK, it's interesting that everything has been fine at home, because in school… / Ah well, it's interesting that things have been hard at home, as we've seen a similar pattern in school.

Let parents start

I think it is proper etiquette to let parents begin by expressing their concerns. Many parents come into school with much anxiety and much to say. Because of this, they are unlikely to be able to hear you until they have downloaded their perspective. Sometimes parents will refuse to go first – they'll want to listen to what you have to say for yourself – in which case (and if this moment feels hostile), be sure to start and make clear that you are going to be seeking their view of things also.

I often find that when parents go first, they have a very clear view of what has happened, and their minds have often gone to the worst possible outcome. In these situations (and when you feel you haven't yet reached the end of the road), problem-solving is much more comfortable.

Sometimes parents make you aware of things that have been going on in school that you have no awareness of. It is good to get misconceptions out of the way from the get-go, so that you don't end up with egg on your face.

Take notes that you can share at the end. Note-taking means that you are not left with an impression of what occurred, it demonstrates that you are serious about transparency, and it gives everyone a jumping-off point for action plans.

Hold the space

When people talk about holding space, it can often seem like one of those techniques that people nod sagely about but that no one understands. However, I believe holding space is one of the most important techniques a leader can rely on in their toolkit.

Holding space is a skill that all good coaches learn, and it is a skill that I use when I am working with parents through breakthrough conversations, and when I am doing the same with young people.

Holding space requires you to have unconditional positive regard for the human being you are with and, at the same time, to feel a kind of emptiness of mind that allows what is shared to be untainted by your thoughts and feelings. It requires the deep listening that we talked about in the section on coaching skills in Chapter 5, page 52.

Holding space also requires you to be able to be comfortable with 'what is' and not try to fight it. Thus, if a parent comes in and is furious with you or the school because you have failed them or their child, holding space means you need to be able to recognise that this is 'what is' for this parent. For the moments that they are sharing their information, you must try not to fight it or argue with it, as that then puts you and your emotions into the mix.

When you hold space for another person, they can feel your stability, and they can sense when you lose your confidence. Often, as a coach, this happens when you find yourself immersed in a response or you feel slighted, or indeed when you find what they are saying upsetting.

To maintain stability, you need to be present with your feelings and be conscious about managing them. This takes practice, but the more you can practise holding space for others, the more significant your impact will be in these breakthrough conversations.

Be conscious of your language

All of the above should support you in intentional use of language. However much you feel frustrations bubbling up, if you are committed to having a breakthrough meeting with a parent, you must lead through the difficult stages of the conversation with affirmative speech and an affirmative mind.

Sarcasm is incredibly hostile and yet I have heard teaching professionals use it. Cynicism of any kind has no place in this type of meeting. Indeed, you should choose the most accessible and non-judgemental language you can find to make these conversations with parents move your relationship with them and their trust in your school to a new level.

Recap the conversation

When all parties have had an opportunity to speak about their concerns, you should read the notes back to the assembled attendees, ensuring that the parent's worries and viewpoints have been included.

The meeting should then conclude with a resolution. This can b[e]
or agreed goals if appropriate, or this could be to set out in writi[ng]
review points and meeting dates for these.

These kinds of meetings can be very intense, and they need t[o]
effectively to ensure that you and the parents are not left with a sen[se]
left hanging. Consciously changing the energy at the end of the meet[ing means]
you need to draw attention to the need to move on. So, you might say:

School leader: Thanks again for coming in today. I am really glad that by the end
of the meeting we were able to agree on some clear next steps. Now, what have
you got planned for the rest of the day?

Then finish with affirmatives. This means that your body language, your firm
handshake and the tone of your voice signal that all is well as people prepare
to leave.

Have supervision or a debrief

I always, always recommend that headteachers and leaders have their own coach,
precisely because we hold so many situations and emotions as a container for
others. Teachers getting ground down by meetings with parents is a contributing
factor to them leaving the profession, and I recommend that schools have
supervision processes to support teachers after these meetings. If you don't have
a coach and you are not in a school role where you have been assigned some
supervision, then seek out a trusted colleague and ask them whether they are
prepared to do a debrief with you. To keep things really simple, frame your debrief
with the question 'How did it go?' and then ask your colleagues to support you in
analysing how your breakthrough conversation went.

Headteacher case study

One headteacher I spoke to described a breakthrough conversation with the
parents of a child who had started in her school in Year 7.

When the child started at the school he was living with his father and his
father's partner as well as their other children. He had been taken out of the care
of his mother because she was recovering from substance misuse.

The headteacher described a very calm first six months of the boy being at the
school. His dad backed the school up and upheld the decisions the school tended
to take and was always available to come into school when needed.

However, after these six months, the boy's mother returned to his life. He had a powerful bond with his mum, and he was initially allowed to see her for short periods. The headteacher's breakthrough meeting came when she convened a meeting between Mum, Dad and the social worker, in which the outcome, she hoped, would be that contact with Mum could be agreed in a way that met the needs of the child and did not create chaos.

The meeting started at 5.30 pm and soon descended into volatility. Mum and Dad were angry and could not agree, and the boy, who was present in the meeting, ended up throwing his mobile phone across the room in a rage and then running away, out of the meeting and out of the school.

For the next hour, amid the family's vulnerability, the headteacher searched the nearby housing estate for the boy, who was eventually found.

A few things happened after this meeting. The relationship with the boy's father deteriorated and, indeed, the boy decided that he wanted to return to living with his mother. However, the relationship between the school and the boy's mother moved into a new realm. From this moment on, come what may, the mother was entirely on board with the school. Despite suffering from her own mental health problems, she would come into school whenever bid, and if, for health reasons, she didn't feel able to go into the school, she would make sure that her partner attended on her behalf. When the school introduced a new behaviour policy, this mum got on board and read the literature that had informed the policy in order that she could support her son as best she could at home. Whenever there was an issue at home, she would email the headteacher and let her know what had happened so that the school could pre-empt issues. In short, she was utterly on board because she had been treated like a human being by a school leader in her hour of need.

Sadly, at the beginning of Year 8, the behaviour of the boy escalated. Things were not going well at home or in school. One day, the head had to take the unfortunate decision to exclude the boy permanently.

Because of the relationship that the parent had with the headteacher, it came as no surprise to this mum that this moment had come. As painful as it was for everyone involved, there was no pushback. What was clear was that the school had been working side by side with the family throughout it all.

After the PEX hearing, the headteacher realised just how much she had become a vital support to this parent. The mother sought her counsel about how she was going to get through the next phase of ensuring her child settled in the new school. She also sought her advice on how she would now cope on a personal level.

What happens when the conversation does not go well?

I am very aware that we often share the stories of our success in books like this and we share case studies of situations in which everything has worked out well. However, there are occasions when things don't go as we would like, yet the conversation could still be considered to be a breakthrough one.

The following case study, from my own experience, is the anatomy of a meeting that didn't go as well as could have been expected.

Following a series of disastrous meetings with pastoral leaders and a member of the SLT, I was asked to meet the parent of a child who was struggling to manage his behaviour in school.

I had met the parent once before in a back-to-school meeting following a fixed-term exclusion, and he had been accompanied by his wife, who had done most of the talking. The meeting hadn't been hostile, but I could tell that he hadn't thought much of me.

The child held some views that the pastoral team felt came from his dad. This young man would often say, 'Dad says X or Y', and use this as a reason to continue to behave in ways that breached the school behaviour policy and expectations we had of our students. But, because of things he said about race, I knew that his dad certainly held negative views about my being the headteacher and a black woman.

This meeting was particularly challenging. I had had a complaint about an alleged incident of racial abuse from the boy in question. The incident had apparently taken place during a sporting fixture at another school. The claim had come from a headteacher colleague, and a child at her school was the alleged victim.

It took a few hours of interviewing children who had attended the fixture, speaking with staff who had been at the fixture and gathering the notes that my headteacher colleague had taken to establish that, on the balance of probability, this young man had been racially abusive to his opponent.

The boy quibbled on the word usage, but I had determined that there needed to be an appropriate sanction and, along with my PE colleagues, we decided that he would spend the rest of the season 'on the bench'.

Sport was this boy's passion and also his dad's passion, so I knew that delivering the news of the sanction would be tricky. The meeting with his dad couldn't have started worse. He was incandescent with rage, and it took a good 30 minutes for him to reach the point of being able to talk and not shout, point or otherwise gesticulate inappropriately.

I needed to use every tool in my coaching toolkit to stay calm and feel safe, and I did this through presence, stillness in the face of aggression and breathing. I breathed slowly and calmly and kept reiterating that I wanted to hear his views but that it would be easier to do this if he would stop shouting.

When he eventually did calm down, I moved the conversation out of the micro of the match ban and the specifics of whether or not the abuse had been racially motivated and into the macro of sports leadership and the movement to kick racism out of sport. Interestingly, his views on race blurred when it came to talking about black sporting heroes and I wonder how much his prejudice towards me was based on me being a woman and not my blackness.

To my relief, I had hit upon a topic that resonated for him, and we then spent 15 minutes or so talking about what we both agreed young people learned through sport – leadership, collaboration and so forth.

I am a great people person, and I enjoy finding out what makes people tick. I pieced together the dad's views on sport in education, and he opened up about standards of behaviour from his school days versus the present day. He also talked about a number of his personal struggles. I was empathetic and held the space, as I knew that this was an essential factor in him learning to trust the school.

Feeling that I was now on stable ground to circle back and remind him that what we had been talking about was the reason why I was issuing a rest-of-season ban, I did just that.

However, on this occasion, it just did not work. Usually, I am confident that a moment of togetherness, sharing the bird's eye view of the situation, will bring parents to an agreement regarding the proposed consequences for poor behaviour. This dad, however, just immediately saw red. In fact, his interpretation of us moving the conversation towards common ground was that he had softened me. He was outraged that 'after the chat we had just had, I was not minded to drop this match ban'.

I held my ground, kept breathing, kept steady and reiterated that I was glad we were both in agreement about the need for a sanction given the situation, and then was grateful that my PA arrived to tell me that my next meeting had come.

Now it seems in this case study that no breakthrough occurred. It could look like the dad thought he was winning me over and then, when he didn't get his own way, that we were no further forward.

However, it is not quite the case. Interestingly, that was the last time that the dad came into school shouting and raging. This man had gone from being a regular threatening feature who staff were reluctant to talk to for fear he would march into reception demanding to see them, to a parent who handed responsibility for dealing with the school to his wife.

I didn't see him again. I wonder if it was because the conversation created a dynamic he wasn't comfortable with but, whatever it was, the conversation changed things for us all.

Anatomy of a parent meeting

We sometimes have parents who are like our kryptonite, and we have to engage all of our self-management skills to be able to work with them.

I had met with this particular parent on several occasions before her child started at the school and I was confident that we were on the same page with regard to how the school would work to support her child's needs. However, as the first year progressed, it was clear that her expectations were much higher than we would be able to meet, and every meeting and phone call with her became increasingly stressful.

This mother would shout and rage at me; she would threaten calling the press, the local authority and her MP. Each time I would approach the matter with a calm insistence, but our relationship had become antagonistic, and I often felt stressed about and wary of meeting her.

In one multi-professional meeting, I remember seeing her as an angry cat who was trapped. She was surrounded by professionals who she felt were doing nothing to support her and her family and whom she had ostracised as a result of the way she talked to and treated them. I so wanted to do more to help her, but my ego got the better of me at times, and I found myself in an immovable situation, one in which she would not budge, and I would not alter my expectations of her conduct.

One day, things changed. I decided to go into a meeting with her taking the perspective that the school and I had not gotten her and her family the support we would have wanted them to have. I was going to acknowledge fully and open-heartedly that we had gotten some things wrong. I was going to try to drop all defensiveness, however hard she pushed.

I went into that meeting so hellbent on my big statement of responsibility that I failed her yet again. Hearing me and 'my platitudes' didn't help her and, in fact, it incensed her. I sat back in my chair glumly staring down the barrel of another long meeting in which tempers would no doubt fray and hostility would ensue.

But then I began to listen. I let this mother speak and be heard, probably for the first time in our relationship. I heard her without any defensiveness, without any rage, without any feeling of slight. I was quietly affirming her as her broken sentences threatened my understanding. I encouraged her to tell me more of the past and of how events had led us to this place. I listened to the pain she was going through, her anxieties for her children, her sense of not being good enough. I listened to the let-downs she had experienced over successive years, as school after school had failed her child, and as the family had tried to navigate the system.

I can't think why it had taken me so long to hear this mother, but it had, and once I eventually did hear her, I felt nothing but compassion.

Our relationship shifted from that meeting onward. We did not resolve the fact that she felt the school was not doing enough, but the bottom line was that she knew her objections to our work and her determination for certain things to be put in place had been heard.

Years later I bumped into this mother. She embraced me in the middle of a shop and told me that she was so sorry for the way things had been between us. She apologised for some of her behaviour and said she felt embarrassed, looking back, at some of the things that had happened. I told her that there was no embarrassment needed. I had been present during a particular season of her family's life, a difficult one. We had all learned something in that time. As a consequence of my relationship with her, I had realised my role as a leader was to hold the space for another human being confidently. My job was to hold space without fear or threat and with ego to the side. The experience had taught us both.

*

This chapter has explored the importance of being able to manage and conduct successful meetings with parents. It has given a step-by-step framework for teachers and leaders who want to get better at holding meetings with parents, as well as a number of case studies of parent meetings to reassure leaders and parents that parent meetings can go any number of ways, all of which can lead to a positive conclusion.

Key questions to help you light the way

1. Does your school create a culture in which staff feel comfortable having breakthrough conversations with parents?

2. Are staff in your school skilled at preparing and managing these conversations?

3. Are there things your school could do to make the format of meetings like these more comfortable for parents?

4. Has your school considered the need for supervision for staff who manage lots of these types of conversations with parents?

5. How can we encourage every leader to demonstrate the courage and integrity to 'sit in the fire' with parents in times of challenge? How can you light the way towards this?

14 Compassionate engagement with families

Chapter overview

This chapter sets out some of the transformative effects on the school community when we are intentional about parental engagement. It explores the need for compassion when working with parents. It goes on to consider the types of parental engagement that could encourage a greater diversity of parents into the school. Why? Because to light the way in challenging times we need leaders who recognise the role they have in bringing *everyone* with them and who have the tools to encourage buy-in from diverse groups.

I could have made the meeting outlined in the previous chapter a situation in which I developed an antipathy towards parent meetings. Still, I genuinely think we add more value to the world when we use these situations to get better at our art of human relating.

It can be tricky to feel this way, and many teachers suffer from challenging relationships with parents. Schools must, therefore, do everything they can to try to ensure that the culture of their school fosters good relations with parents. This supports all members of the school community.

In a study conducted by researchers at Bath Spa University in 2017, in which nearly 10,000 teachers were polled, it was found that a third of teachers had suffered abuse from parents at some point. It also found that within that month, 28 per cent of primary teachers, 18 per cent of secondary teachers and 15 per cent of teaching assistants had been the victims of abuse or challenging behaviour from parents, either online or on school premises (Bloom, 2017).

I have worked in schools in which the impact of abusive parents has had to be very carefully managed, as inexperienced teachers, in particular, found the overstepping of boundaries and excessive demands of some parents understandably challenging.

I have also needed to manage some extremely challenging, litigious and potentially harmful behaviour by parents. As a headteacher, I became accustomed, in recent years, to the regular stream of letters, sometimes complaints and certainly concerns, that would be addressed to me as the head, and have felt the unrelenting nature of parents' expectations.

However, I don't see these as negative developments. Certainly, there are issues with how some parents communicate, but I think we must be cautious about fearing the greater levels of empowerment that many parents now have. I think we should be pleased that we are working in an era in which deference has been edged out in favour of provocation and that more and more parents see their place in improving the school experience for their child.

The hostility with which some teachers talk about parental behaviour demeans our profession. Articles with titles like '11 types of parents that teachers secretly dislike' don't help. Indeed, this tone, which aspects of the media support, of belittling so-called 'helicopter parents', as well as demeaning those who are not involved in school life, is a reminder of how uncomfortable I used to find the staffroom in the early days of teaching.

When I first started teaching, I worked in a context in which it was clear that many teachers felt that they were doing the kids and the community a favour by being there. There were pockets of teachers who had outright hostile views towards parents, and talk of smelly families and jokes about fumigating rooms after parent meetings were rife. Some teachers would laugh at the improbability of Parent X ever making it to school for a parent meeting, and others would think that meant that large numbers of parents in the school didn't care about their child's school journey. There were teachers who had worked in the school for many years, so judgements about certain families went deep. They had taught some of the parents and had hostile relationships with some of them that spanned several years. Their thoughts about certain families failed to allow any room for change, growth or the maturation of the relationship. I was dismayed by these judgements; I was horrified at the hostility, as it spoke to my deepest anxieties about the nature of power and about the danger of how institutions wield that power in damaging ways if left unchecked.

Who's engaging whom?

There are many reasons why some parents don't get as involved as we might like them to and many reasons why some parents get more involved than we would like them to. But before we look at them, we need to explore our preference as school leaders to seek this one true and perfect type of parental engagement.

In my opinion, schools should really spend time thinking about the reasons why they want parental engagement because it can mean different things. Indeed, the terms 'parental involvement' and 'parental engagement' are used almost interchangeably but seem to have different functions and require a different set of activities to occur.

Parental engagement is defined by the National Improvement Hub (Education Scotland, 2019) as being 'the involvement of parents in supporting their children's academic learning'. While a 'broad interpretation of parental engagement is adopted by the Department for Education', this includes 'learning at home, school–home and home–school communication, in-school activities, decision-making (e.g. being a parent governor) and collaborating with the community' (Department for Education, 2011). Parental involvement is cited in an Education Scotland report as 'representing many different parental behaviours; parenting practices such as parental aspirations for their child's academic achievement; parental communication with their children about school; parental participation in school activities; parental communications with teachers about their child; and parental rules at home which are considered to be education-related' (Education Scotland, 2018).

What is startling about these definitions to me is that they both seem to put the onus on parents to be the agents. It is the parents who must fit in with the school's determination of how they can best help their child with learning, and it is the set of activities determined by the school that the parent is expected to become involved in. What neither of these approaches seem to prioritise genuinely is what parents need. These approaches do not make that much of the efforts that schools must make to do the engaging.

The reasons why parents don't always engage

Some parents are afraid to come into school and be involved. For many parents, there is a fear of engaging in discussions about their child's learning. This is because they probably don't want to hear that they or their child are considered by the school to somehow be at fault. When I worked in the pupil referral service, one of the things that struck me was just how many times most of our parents had been called into school or phoned only to receive the bad news that their child had done something wrong. Again.

For many parents, there is a fear of having to lose a day's work to come and pick up their child from school. There is a fear that their child might be excluded permanently, and they don't want to face this news. For some, there is the fear that they can't manage a spiralling situation. This all means that they will avoid your phone calls and your letters inviting them into school. It also means that they will certainly avoid the potential humiliation of sitting in a hall full of beaming and proud parents at parents' evening to be told by successive teachers that their child is not meeting the mark.

Some parents fear that they are not able to support their child's learning. For many immigrant parents I worked with in the early 2000s, learning the English language was a barrier that they were working to overcome, but they were not there yet. A fear that they were missing essential information and would hinder and not be able to help their child was genuine.

Some parents had terrible experiences at school. They have coped with their lack of basic skills in their adult life, but unstructured or open home-learning support tasks terrify them.

Other parents simply don't have time. Many parents are in full-time work and are unable to find time during the school day to attend meetings. Parents' evenings that start at 4.30 pm and finish at 7.30 pm are going to be a struggle for any parent with a long commute or who is a shift worker. And no, taking time off is not an option for many parents, just as it isn't an option for most teachers to take unpaid leave to attend an event in their child's school.

The problem might also be that parents don't know what is expected of them and why. Many schools hold events, the etiquette of which is shrouded in mystery. As a socially confident school leader, I struggle in all sorts of ways when attending events. I hate not knowing the way an event is going to be organised or what the expectation of me will be. There is something I find so rude about not having the forethought to explain the exact expectations of parents at events like parents' evening and yet how many of us do this on a recurring and consistent basis? How many of us think about how we can build the trust and resilience of our community of parents and get them engaging in the world of the school from a position of confidence?

What's working now in parental engagement?

I've been in leadership roles where I feel we've definitely gotten parental engagement right and others where we really haven't done as well.

The schools in which it was successful incorporated several strategies that made sure that parents felt like active partners and, because of the context of the school, were particularly suitable.

What now follows is a series of tips to support leaders who want to develop parental engagement in their schools.

1. Getting involved in the community

In my experience, living and working in the community my school served brought benefits and occasional challenges. One of the more significant benefits was that it enabled greater ease of participation in community events as they were often right on my doorstep.

Regardless of how near or far you or your staff live from the school, engaging in community leadership and events is an excellent way of ensuring that the community know and feel your interest in them. Likewise, being a governor in a school local to you, supporting parents' charitable efforts or patronising their businesses can send a similar message.

2. Communicating effectively

The reason why I keep coming back to communication is that it is so easily overlooked and, in my experience, so easy to get wrong. I have had varying degrees of success with parental communications and have accepted that electronic bulletins with information that is gathered by various members of the school community and centrally collated work best.

I prefer face-to-face communication as less is left open to misinterpretation, but that is often a challenge in huge schools with thousands of parents to communicate with!

Written communications don't work for some parents, and so thinking through which translation services might be needed, what can be sent by text, what should go out by email and which parents might require a quick call or face-to-face briefing or meeting is critical.

I have worked in schools in which parent representatives assisted with the dissemination of information in each class and, in so doing, supported the class teachers hugely. These roles required a lot of forethought and a carefully constructed job description, but they were worth it.

3. Getting the balance right at parent events

Different members of the school community want and need different things to feel engaged and welcomed, so getting parent events right can be tricky.

Parents' evenings will support and engage many parents but will alienate others, particularly if they do not know how to help their child, or their child is not doing so well. Having more bespoke opportunities for these identified parents to talk through academic achievement may well enable them to cross the threshold.

Social events can be intimidating at the best of times, and adult school communities have cliques as much as student ones do. Encourage parents who may otherwise be on the periphery, or not feel comfortable attending school barbecues, fairs or coffee mornings, to become part of the organising team. Having a role can help focus their involvement and ensures they are anchored to the event and not left to shuffle awkwardly in a corner or not attend at all.

Demonstrating how we work as schools and explaining clearly what parents can do to help their children with schoolwork is some of the best work we can do to engage parents. Again, a balance between events that elucidate an aspect of the curriculum or a process and support for wider parenting issues is excellent. Thus, schools should balance a Year 9 'Options' evening, with classes for parents focused on supporting their child's mental health or awareness of how to support a child through adolescence. This demonstrates that the school wants to help parents in their parenting efforts as much as it wants support from parents to achieve its academic aims.

How to create a culture of compassion when working with parents

It is worth recognising that the community of the school is far broader than the current set of children and their families. Very often, past parents, future parents, community members and school neighbours want to weigh in on school issues, and rightly so. In these cases, compassion is needed in the way we approach stakeholder and parental engagement. We need to ensure that we have school mechanisms that are genuinely not judgemental and encourage a diversity of voices to be heard – yes, even difficult ones.

One of the more challenging aspects of school leadership I engaged with in recent years was the introduction of a new school uniform. We did consult on the changes to the uniform, and we had a reasonable response, with the majority of parents believing that changes to the uniform would be a good thing. However, a broad group of stakeholders in and beyond the school were very unhappy that the school would take this decision.

Several outraged, sometimes rude but often well-argued, letters ensued. I was very aware that the way the issue was handled would speak volumes about the school if

I didn't take the opportunity to invite parents in to talk to me about their objections. So, I did. With representation from a number of parents who held differing views, I facilitated a consultation evening where I listened to and heard everyone.

The power of listening was transformative and previously enflamed emotions were extinguished in a couple of hours as parents shared their views and heard those of members of the school team. We all left with a better understanding of each other but also with an affirmation that, regardless of our thoughts on the issue at hand, we all wanted the school to be successful. I share this example to illustrate that, although school matters can often feel of paramount importance and although it can feel that we must at all costs maintain control of how these matters unfold, it is sometimes helpful to loosen the reins of control and adjust our course. It shows humility but is usually yet another opportunity for growth.

Don't judge, practise 'upekkha'

Complete non-judgement is probably impossible; we all have biases and conditioning that arise in an instant at will and in most situations. However, 'upekkha' is a Buddhist practice of finding equanimity or non-attachment, and this can be found daily. Maintaining equanimity is a brilliant leadership tool that anyone can master. It is totally free, and it has the power to transform the most challenging of situations.

There are situations of parental abuse and parental neglect that make non-attachment very challenging, of course. But, thankfully, the majority of occurrences in school in which we take a judgemental stance can be tackled with an attitude of compassion, in the space between praise and blame.

We often don't know or understand all that much about children's lives at home, although it can sometimes feel like we do. And, despite the feeling that we spend all the time with them, children actually spend only about 20 per cent of this time with us. The other hours are spent in the care of their parents.

I once had to deal with a situation in which a troubled boy was working his way through the behaviour stages of the school, and there were serious concerns that he would end up being permanently excluded. Before I had met his mother, I became aware of her in the way that staff members talked about her. There was a rolling of eyes about the fact that she was unlikely to come into school, as she worked and often worked away. I fed into this and recall vividly having to check myself and my own judgements.

What was so fascinating about this particular situation was that she, like I, was a mother to a mixed-race boy; she, like I, worked in a leadership role; she, like I, had to spend many hours away from home; and she, like I, had entrusted the care of her child to a broader community family group.

We are told it takes a village to raise a child but, if I was able to fall into the easy trap of judging a woman for not being able to come into a school meeting because she was working, what hope was there?

For all the differences that we choose to focus on, most people are pretty much the same. We have systems of what is right and wrong, and we none of us think we are doing a good enough job. We try to escape pain and run towards relief, and we would be hard-pressed not to find some resonance of our own behaviours in the behaviours of others.

Don't be hostile

There can be a lot of hostility when people talk about parents or the local community. Usually, those sentences that begin 'The trouble with our parents is…' are not sentences that end well. The hostile lumping together of all parents or locals demonstrates a lack of willingness to engage with individual concerns.

I believe our thoughts determine our feelings, which determine our behaviours. Talking cynically or unkindly about parents on social media, in the staffroom or at home with your friends and family further fuels your negative thinking and feelings towards 'parents' and allows an otherness to creep in.

Fat-shaming is an example I'll use, as it is often delivered as though it is harmless fun. I have had to call out colleagues who would leave a dramatic pause around descriptions of parents who are overweight or who would smirk at the inability of a whole family to manage excessive weight. These comments are made from a sense of superiority and otherness, and they suggest a hostility towards those who can be guaranteed to be already giving themselves a hard-enough time about their difficult relationship with health. I can assure you, they do not need further fuel from teachers and school leaders.

Inner work is at the heart of our ability to cultivate compassion over hostility. All it takes is commitment.

Be respectful

I can't think of many occasions on which a local authority advisor, a school improvement advisor or an Ofsted inspector would come into school and be made to wait in reception for an excessive length of time. I can't think of a time when a governor would come into school commenting about their busy morning and explaining that they had rushed from their last appointment to get to school and they were not offered a drink. So, I cannot fathom why parents are sometimes mistreated when they come into school and why simple courtesy can sometimes go out of the window.

Coming into school for a discussion around challenging topics like a child's behaviour or possible exclusion, about a pastoral support plan or any kind of review meeting is incredibly stressful for parents. It can be made so much more comfortable with the offer of a cup of tea, checking to see whether anyone wants to use the loo before the meeting begins and making sure that the reception staff have had the heads-up that Mrs X is coming in for a meeting and she needs to be shown some extra-special warmth when she arrives.

The way we treat parents needs to be run through the sense-check of the school's values. If anything is out of alignment, it needs fixing.

Develop trust

It can be taken for granted that you have a child or the school's best interests at heart, but it is one of those things that needs reiterating over and over. Developing the trust that you are coming from the right place and that you want to build a strong school for the community helps no end.

Trust is built through consistent and regular communication, especially when things are challenging. It is essential as school leaders that we show we are trustworthy through admitting to things that have not gone well. If communication has broken down or been insufficient, then leaders must take steps to make amends but also own up to their mistakes.

Listening is an underrated leadership skill but again an important one when it comes to building trust with our community. Listening requires us to be patient and to lose our defensiveness about situations.

*

Through patient listening and openness to the views, needs and hopes of our school and local communities, school leaders make the transition to community leaders. The backing of the local community will strengthen you when times are tough. As this chapter has demonstrated, trust can be cultivated through a commitment to leading ethically beyond the school gates.

Key questions to help you light the way

1. How effectively does your school engage all parents?

2. Have you run your parental engagement efforts through the lens of values?

3. Have you got the balance right between parent meetings that support parenting and parent meetings that support academic achievement?

4. How can you support your staff in non-judgement when working with parents?

5. How can we ensure that every parent, regardless of context, feels actively embraced and engaged in the life of the school? How can you light the way towards this?

15 Changing the system

Chapter overview

This chapter sets out how to work beyond your school gates to bring about change. It considers the power and benefit of articulating the challenges faced by the sector as a means of transforming it. It argues for the amplification of voices and experiences in order that we can envision a better future together. Why? Because to light the way in challenging times we need leaders who will speak the stories of their journeys and, in so doing, encourage others to start out on epic journeys of their own.

When I was asked by my CEO how I would feel about participating in a documentary series being made about the school system, I was at first a little nervous about the idea. I hate reality TV, and I couldn't imagine that a fly-on-the-wall series would do much to add to the knowledge of those not working within the school system. But we met with the producers and slowly my belief that this could be an opportunity to share my views about what was working and what was not working in the system for both children and adults was strengthened.

I was very conscious during the filming of *School* that I wanted to model ethical leadership, and this meant the cameras needed to capture the multitude of tasks and responsibilities I had as an interim headteacher and not just the good bits. That wasn't hard. My year at The Castle School encompassed financial woes, SEND provision cuts and a restructuring of teaching and learning responsibilities, as well as management of buildings and premises in a dire state of repair. I hoped that in filming a leader not always getting it right, but trying nevertheless to do the right thing, people would see into the complexities of work in a system navigating difficult and complicated social times.

The footage was at times bleak, but I found it remarkable that the objections that were made to the depictions we gave of our school experience suggested a 'talking up of teaching' should prevail.

I have found no benefit in avoiding the truth of circumstance in favour of positive spin. There are plenty of schools doing brilliantly well and in which staff are happy, but to suggest that we shouldn't speak up and out in schools that are struggling is nonsense and it is a premise I have sought to challenge. Believing, as I do, that we share our experiences to normalise them for other people and to take the pressure off others is the reason I agreed to bare all in the series *School*.

I stuck to my guns, and I was overwhelmed by the communications from teachers who were also finding things tough. There were teachers who reached out to me who were grateful that there was some acknowledgement that things are very hard right now. And there were teachers across the country who also, like me, wouldn't want to be involved in any other profession. What united us was that we love education, we wanted to work in it, and we wanted it to get better.

The following contribution is from James Pope. He was a headteacher friend and colleague who also featured in the documentary *School* and what he has gone on to do illustrates what I mean when I talk about the benefits that can come from sharing our stories and being open about the struggles of working in schools.

Thoughts from a head who left (on TV), by James Pope

A little while ago, I completed a strengths analysis as part of some positive psychology training I was undertaking. Hope is my top strength, followed by love, creativity and fairness. I was mildly disappointed that leadership was seventh in the list but perhaps I shouldn't have been that surprised given my experience of headship.

I am 'accidentally passionate' about education – accidentally because it was never a career ambition, passionate because of my own experiences, including my own failure to take advantage of my education. This accidental passion started in 1997 and has blossomed ever since. A subset of my passion for education is my passion for leadership, specifically school leadership. I realised early on in my teaching career that I could inspire (not always, but occasionally) students through my teaching; through leadership, I could do the same for a whole community. This led me to Marlwood School in 2014.

My first headship was long desired and achieved through hard work and determination. On the interview days, I remember being struck by the sense of loosely controlled chaos. The 'norm' of the behaviour was just the wrong side of 'edgy' and student interactions came with a hint of negativity and spiky wariness of the strange (me). I also had a strong sense of the entire community… waiting, holding its breath, stuck on pause. It was clear that there was a lot to do, but it was also clear that there was a lot going for the place – so I barely missed a beat as I answered 'Yes' to the killer question: 'Do you accept?' With my shield of hope firmly attached to my forearm, I arrived at the start of September 2014.

I've written at some length about the detail of my first three years of headship and the context of the school. Suffice to say: I was correct in thinking there was a lot to do. Much of what needed to be done was significantly hampered by the financial context, which I had been led to believe was stable (it was not). Nevertheless, it was a *lot* of fun; the staff were brilliant and open-minded, and the children and parents were an absolute joy.

Bit by bit, little by little, we were winning. The culture shifted to the right side of 'edgy'; the children and their families bought into what we were doing. Through a mixture of creativity and collaboration, we pretty much rebuilt every system and structure at the school. We played the game in Year 11, but we invested the majority of the resources into Key Stage 3 and a comprehensive curriculum redesign to suit the future size of the school. We were research-led in our strategies, and we looked across the country, through the whole education network, for different ways of designing and developing a future-faced school.

Looking back now, it was a whirlwind two and a half years. During that time, I took an executive head position within the MAT, adding some capacity to the leadership of one of the primary schools. I also became the chair of the secondary headteachers' association (for context, in a small local authority of some 20-plus secondary schools, within one year of headship at Marlwood, I became the third-longest-serving headteacher in the local authority; secondary heads meetings were a regular live version of *Guess Who?*).

My strengths – hope, love, creativity and fairness – stood me in good stead during this time, but they were also nourished and fed by the sense of community that was building around me. I hope that I bring positive energy to the table, but I also need to have that reflected back to me, not through false praise or hollow compliments but through seeing the impact of the work.

After two and a half years, in May 2017, two things happened:

1. We signed up to make the TV series *School*. The trust had been in discussion with a television production company for a few months to make

a television series for BBC Two, highlighting the complexity and challenges faced by schools after a decade of austerity and policy upheaval and the impact that this had had on young people, their families and staff.

2. Ofsted arrived and placed Marlwood in 'special measures'.

My final year of headship in South Gloucestershire, within CSET at Marlwood School, is therefore pretty well documented. The *School* episodes devoted to Marlwood paint a bleak picture. It made for pretty depressing viewing. But it could never capture the full story.

Throughout my career (and indeed as a child and a student), I had spent much of my time looking up to others, in awe of their skill, poise and wisdom, and in doing so very much seeing myself as less worthy than them. Imposter syndrome. This is great from the point of view of always seeing myself as someone with something to learn from others. I have a natural tendency, linked to my strengths, to see the best in others. I trust people.

As a headteacher at Marlwood, while dealing with the bizarre set of circumstances that effectively meant that everything was lined up to make sure the school failed, I increasingly came to realise that some of the others I looked up to, from faceless power brokers in government through to more local individuals with the power to resolve some of the issues we were facing, needed to be challenged. For me, the TV programme was a challenge to the government and more broadly the society that the government reflects. It wasn't political, but the impact of years of austerity on the school system needed to be shown. I wasn't to know when we signed to make *School* that we would be put in special measures shortly afterwards. I certainly wasn't to know that I would end up resigning within 12 months.

Do I regret it? Not one bit.

The reasons I resigned are complex and down to no one particular thing, but the relevant point here is to do with personal conflict. The upshot of Marlwood's financial position and the status that Ofsted projected onto the school was a personal deep-seated unease that I was being pushed to enact a series of 'tactics' and behaviours that were at conflict with my personal values and those that I hold in regard to creating a community bound by a quality education. The very creativity that I had been recruited to bring to the table for the long-term transformation of the school was being systematically dismantled around me in a desperate short-term scrabble to dance to Ofsted's tune.

Over the course of my headship, I'd had a growing sense of unease and conflict with the education system as a whole and the accountability system that is sadly and incorrectly at the vanguard of setting the direction of travel. In conversation with other leaders in other settings, it became obvious that I wasn't the only one to feel this way. I left with the intention of setting up a network of like-minded leaders who, like me, felt that things just aren't 'right'. And so www.inspireducate.co.uk was created to challenge and speak truth to the contradictions and those who uphold them in our system. The creation of the TV programme and the filming of some of my lengthier monologues on the state of education (sadly cut from the final programmes!) had provided me with the confidence to speak up.

In my travels and the work that I am now doing, I am privileged to visit schools all over the country, and I get to speak to school leaders from all sorts of contexts. I am endlessly amazed by the hard work, skill and determination of those who work in our profession to provide the best education that they possibly can for the children who attend their school. There is so much to celebrate and yet we seem to have forgotten how to do that in a way that is detached from the accountability system or the performance indicators.

Out of this was born 'HeadsUp' (@HeadsUp4HTs). A direct consequence of *School* has been a steady stream of contacts from headteachers who describe having left, being made to leave or being in the process of leaving their schools. The circumstances and contexts were different for each of them in many ways. What they had in common was shared anger and upset towards the system. In some cases, they had been on the receiving end of some seriously unethical behaviour on the part of their employer. Some had 'disappeared', while others had got back in. Many can't speak out, muted by non-disclosure agreements, a particularly sinister consequence of the system-wide collusion that celebrates leaders on recruitment and then throws them on the scrap heap, without policy or process, when they haven't solved the unsolvable puzzle in 18 months. HeadsUp is calling it out and shining a light on this issue.

Why it's OK to call out the system

The problem with trying to paper over the cracks in the system, with trying to make out that it is great when so many people feel that it isn't, is that it alienates the very people who are needed in order for it to heal.

So, headteachers and school leaders read stories of schools that are doing really well, they read reports from those who want to talk up the sector and, because they don't recognise their experience of their work, they feel that it must be them who have gotten it wrong. They must somehow be at fault for not enjoying every day, for not coping well with stress and anxiety, and for not having the fantastic results that everyone else has managed to achieve.

Teachers go on to Twitter, and they see pictures of other teachers' classrooms, teachers who have spent the entire summer holiday organising their classroom for the academic year ahead, and they feel inferior and exhausted.

Teachers who are also parents read about the possibilities of co-headship, shared headship and flexible working. Yet others find themselves being penalised for requesting part-time work or flexible working and some even find themselves at threat of losing their job while on maternity leave or for pursuing their ideal working scenario because a school refuses to bend and flex.

It is great to talk up teaching. It is a fantastic profession and it is a privilege to work in schools, but that doesn't mean that we cannot acknowledge that certain things don't work and haven't been working for a great many young people and staff in a great many schools.

Some teachers are stressed, some leaders are at breaking point, and many educators are leaving the profession. Budgets are stretched too thin in many schools. Buildings and premises do not meet our hopes for every child, and children in many, many schools do not meet our national expected standard. This is a standard that indicates that a good education has been given and received. To say these things is not disloyal to the profession. It is honest, and honesty allows people the chance to take stock of their lot and make a change for the better.

Speaking up about the profession need not be negative. It could simply be factual, and I believe from that factual, 'emotionally objective' standpoint, we would find ourselves much better equipped to find solutions.

If we apply the African philosophy of Ubuntu to the profession, we would see that we have a long way to go. Ubuntu is often translated as 'I am because we are'. As it relates to the world of schools and the education system, it means we, as a profession, are as strong as our weakest members.

This means that headteachers as a group are as strong as the one of us who lies awake at three o'clock in the morning worrying about the future of their livelihood and their school.

This means that teachers as a group are as strong as the teacher who can't face turning their car into the car park and instead sits and sobs outside the school gates.

This means that schools are as well-equipped as the school with leaking roofs and not enough money to fund resources for the classroom.

This means that as a nation the success of our children can only meaningfully be celebrated through the lens of those who left school with nothing, not a single GCSE to their name.

This is not talking down teaching; this is a call-out to galvanise the profession around a set of truths that we have the power to turn around.

Speak out to save the profession

I have seen so many teachers and educator writers recently preface their writing, which expresses concern for teachers and the profession, with 'I believe in the education system', as though terrified they will be called out for their negativity. But I argue for speaking up and speaking out. I urge all teachers and leaders to take to the airwaves with the courage to share your stories. Share your stories now, while you are in post. Gather together and normalise the experience of being an educator for another person. Feel the transformative effects of speaking up and being brave. It is in your truths that we will find solutions to the current difficulties, and it is in owning these truths that you can have a transformative effect on your own mental health and wellbeing and those of fellow professionals.

Practical steps you can take to speak up and save the profession

Below are some practical ways in which you, as an individual, can express your thoughts and feelings about the profession, with the aim of speaking out to make things better for both yourself and your colleagues.

Get off the fence

It can be intimidating to get your voice out there and stand for something but, while you hang back, there are others making a much louder case for maintaining the status quo of the system or advocating much more worrying routes. If something doesn't work about the way schools are run, about accountability mechanisms, or about workload, wellbeing or a multitude of other aspects of school life, say something about it and put forward your solutions – light another way! It's surprising, once you start to stand for something, just how many people will want to stand with you.

Start to blog

Blogging is great for your own mental health and a brilliant vehicle to chew over ideas and share your thoughts with peers. Blogging about your experiences in education will doubtless resonate with another person, working in another school somewhere across the land, and it is in these resonances that people find great comfort but also the energy to spark change.

Speak on a stage

From TEDx Talks to local TeachMeets, there are a host of opportunities for teachers and leaders to get their voices heard from the stage. Events like BrewEd, CollectiveEd and ResearchEd can offer a platform, as can unconferences and conferences like the WomenEd and BAMEed events.

Use the power of social media

We need to be cautious in our use of social media in order that we don't bring the profession, our schools or ourselves into disrepute. That said, if you have some clear views that might spark debate and discussion on social media and that might lend support to a movement wanting to disrupt the current narrative, then offer them up. There are a range of platforms on which to do this. The vast EduTwitter sphere is remarkably rich in ideas and debate and, who knows, you putting yourself out there could lend some helpful thought leadership on an issue that others have been grappling with.

Write a book

If your thought leadership has reached the stage of being more well-rounded, you might be ready to share it with a wider audience. There are a number of education publishers who are ready to hear your thoughts on changing the education system and there really is no excuse not to send in a book proposal and see what they think of your idea.

*

This chapter has explored some of the ways in which leaders can use their voices to lead change in the education sector beyond the school gates. It provides a case study of one headteacher who, having left headship, has gone on to lift the lid on the numerous pressures facing headteachers and to find ways of supporting them. The chapter then offers a number of practical strategies to support you in finding your voice and leading change beyond your school.

Key questions to help you light the way

1. How confident do you feel in speaking out about some of the challenges facing our schools?
2. How can you demonstrate courage and use your leadership voice beyond the school to restore faith in the system?
3. How can you master the art of speaking positively in the face of challenges? No. Matter. What.
4. How can we encourage all leaders to light their own way and speak the stories of their journeys?

Final thoughts

I wrote this book as a means of adding a new narrative to the ones we have on education leadership in schools. I wanted to elucidate some of the skills that I think are needed by school leaders to address school life in these incredibly challenging times. This is because I believe it is through ethical school leadership that we can usefully bring the power of compassion, dignity and integrity to bear. The book has sought to demonstrate that there is a way of engaging with all of the issues that arise in our schools – inclusion, exclusion, behaviour and parental engagement – that prioritises and respects the human being.

There are, of course, many challenges present for children growing up in modern Britain and these challenges extend to their families too. The impact that poverty has on the lives of many of our children is profound; austerity has played a part in making day-to-day existence very hard for these families. Schools must position themselves to provide support and assistance. School staff are not immune to these same challenges as they navigate life, and at the same time, deal with the stress and the workload imbalance that are present. As school leaders, we need to acknowledge that we have the power to impact on our colleagues' wellbeing and abilities to cope positively but that this takes considered and brave action. In schools, we, therefore, find ourselves in a melting pot in which it is unsurprising that certain things bubble over.

In this climate, ethical leadership is vital. School leaders must be torchbearers, leading their staff, students and their local communities with moral purpose. To do this, we need to commit to knowing ourselves and being comfortable with ourselves. We need to address our internal tensions, discomforts and personal anxieties by bringing mindful practices to our work, accessing coaching to help us reframe our work and being very present with our needs. Another part of this is cultivating clarity for the school you are leading and setting out a clear vision for all stakeholders. This means knowing your vision and engaging all the stakeholders in the school in articulating the vision they also see for the community.

Ethical leadership involves leading staff through difficult situations with courage and honesty, and to a greater understanding of themselves. Coaching methods, investing in the development of staff, even when money is scarce, and nurturing autonomy are all essential elements of this. Compassion is also vital if we are to light the way from our current reality to another, better way of doing things. These values must be called upon even when faced with a crisis that needs immediate intervention. The evidence that we have from the profession is that, under pressure, leaders naturally bring their calm authority and dignity to their work. If this could be called upon as the norm and more autonomy offered to leaders to amplify these natural leadership qualities, we would stand a chance of revolutionising the system for the better.

Ethical school leaders must also lead children with moral purpose. There are many ways of working with children that emphasise moral action. From teaching children values through to teaching them about how to behave in ways that mean the school community can function, leaders can model their ethical intentions. Likewise, the way they approach managing exclusions speaks volumes to those intentions.

Finally, it is in our work with parents that we signal to the community beyond the school and to the children within the school that we walk our talk. When we extend our ethical intentions to parents, we amplify our beliefs and exemplify our authenticity.

I hope that readers of this book gain a keen sense of what they can do to add to a narrative of change within the system. Through ethical leadership, we can light the way through the current education system crisis toward a better reality for children, teachers and our society as a whole. With our values of compassion, dignity and integrity in place and the humility of system leaders to acknowledge the journey we must now undertake, we can and will achieve anything we set our minds to.

Bibliography

Ackerman, C. (2019), 'Self-determination theory of motivation: Why intrinsic motivation matters', https://positivepsychology.com/self-determination-theory

All-Party Parliamentary Group on Knife Crime (2019), 'Back to school? Breaking the link between school exclusions and knife crime', www.preventknifecrime.co.uk/wp-content/uploads/2019/10/APPG-on-Knife-Crime-Back-to-School-exclusions-report-FINAL.pdf

Ball, S. (2017), *The Education Debate*. 3rd edn. Bristol: Policy Press.

BAMEed Network, 'About us', www.bameednetwork.com/about-us

Beckford, N. (2015), 'School crime reports topped 30,000 in 2014', BBC News, www.bbc.co.uk/news/education-34268942

Bellis, M. A., Lowey, H., Leckenby, N., Hughes, K. and Harrison, D. (2014), 'Adverse childhood experiences: Retrospective study to determine their impact on adult health behaviours and health outcomes in a UK population', *Journal of Public Health*, 36, (1), 81–91.

Bennett, T. (2017), 'Creating a culture: How school leaders can optimise behaviour', London: Department for Education, https://assets.publishing.service.gov.uk/government/uploads/system/uploads/attachment_data/file/602487/Tom_Bennett_Independent_Review_of_Behaviour_in_Schools.pdf

Bennis, W. (2003), *On Becoming a Good Leader*. 2nd edn. Cambridge: Perseus Publishing.

Bloom, A. (2017), 'A third of teachers have suffered abuse from parents, study shows', *TES*, www.tes.com/news/third-teachers-have-suffered-abuse-parents-study-shows

Boofty, J. (2018), 'I am a teacher and I don't want my children sitting Sats exams', *Independent*, www.independent.co.uk/voices/sats-schools-testing-education-a8294681.html

Bradbury, J. (2019), 'Off-rolling: An update on recent analysis', Ofsted Blog, https://educationinspection.blog.gov.uk/2019/09/06/off-rolling-an-update-on-recent-analysis

Burke, N. J., Hellman, J. L., Scott, B. G., Weems, C. F. and Carrion, V. G. (2011), 'The impact of adverse childhood experiences on an urban pediatric population', *Child Abuse and Neglect*, 35, 408–413.

Callaghan, J. (1976), 'A rational debate based on the facts' (speech). 18 October, Ruskin College, Oxford.

Campbell, D. (2018), 'Sharp rise in young people overdosing on painkillers and antidepressants', *Guardian*, www.theguardian.com/society/2018/sep/11/sharp-rise-in-young-people-overdosing-on-painkillers-and-antidepressants

Centers for Disease Control and Prevention (2019), 'About the CDC–Kaiser ACE Study', www.cdc.gov/violenceprevention/childabuseandneglect/acestudy/about.html

Chetty, R., Hendren, N. and Katz, L. F. (2016), 'The effects of exposure to better neighborhoods on children: New evidence from the moving to opportunity experiment', *American Economic Review*, 106, (4), 855–902.

Cox, E., Bachkirova, T. and Clutterbuck, D. (2018), *The Complete Handbook of Coaching*. 3rd edn. London: Sage.

Crenna-Jennings, W. (2018), 'Key drivers of the disadvantage gap: Literature review. Education in England: Annual Report 2018', London: Education Policy Institute.

Cribb, J., Keiller, A. N. and Waters, T. (2018), 'Living standards, poverty and inequality in the UK: 2018', London: The Institute for Fiscal Studies.

Dalai Lama and Hougaard, R. (2019), 'The Dalai Lama on why leaders should be mindful, selfless, and compassionate', *Harvard Business Review*, https://hbr.org/2019/02/the-dalai-lama-on-why-leaders-should-be-mindful-selfless-and-compassionate

Department for Education (2011), 'Review of best practice in parental engagement', www.gov.uk/government/publications/review-of-best-practice-in-parental-engagement

Department for Education (2017), 'Exclusion from maintained schools, academies and pupil referral units in England', www.gov.uk/government/publications/school-exclusion

Department of Education, 'Dealing with a critical incident', www.education-ni.gov.uk/articles/dealing-critical-incident

Department of Education, 'Suspensions and expulsions', www.education-ni.gov.uk/articles/suspensions-and-expulsions

Di Stefano, G., Gino, F., Pisano, G. P. and Staats, B. R. (2014), 'Making experience count: The role of reflection in individual learning', Harvard Business School Working Paper, No. 14-093.

Duarte, N. and Sanchez, P. (2016), *Illuminate: Ignite change through speeches, stories, ceremonies and symbols*. London: Penguin Random House.

Dutton, J., Lilius, J. and Kanov, J. (2005), 'The transformative potential of compassion at work', in S. K. Piderit, R. E. Fry and D. L. Cooperrider (eds.), *Handbook of Transformative Cooperation: New designs and dynamics*. Stanford, CA: Stanford University Press, pp. 107–126.

Education Endowment Foundation (2019), 'Improving behaviour in schools: Guidance report', https://educationendowmentfoundation.org.uk/tools/guidance-reports/improving-behaviour-in-schools

Education Scotland (2018), 'What is "Parental Involvement" and "Parental Engagement"?', https://education.gov.scot/improvement/research/what-is-parental-involvement-and-parental-engagement

Education Scotland (2019), 'Parental engagement', https://education.gov.scot/improvement/eef-toolkit/parental-engagement

Ethical Leadership Commission (2019), 'Navigating the educational moral maze', www.ascl.org.uk/ASCL/media/ASCL/Our%20view/Campaigns/Navigating-the-educational-moral-maze.pdf

Ferguson, D. (2018), 'Teachers on charity: "It was humbling. I never thought it would happen to me"', *Guardian*, www.theguardian.com/education/2018/jun/26/teachers-on-charity-homeless-hungry

Francis, T. and Hoefel, F. (2018), '"True Gen": Generation Z and its implications for companies', McKinsey and Company, www.mckinsey.com/industries/consumer-packaged-goods/our-insights/true-gen-generation-z-and-its-implications-for-companies

García-Moya, I., Moreno, C. and Brooks, F. M. (2019), 'The "balancing acts" of building positive relationships with students: Secondary school teachers' perspectives in England and Spain', *Teaching and Teacher Education*, 86, 102883.

Gill, K., Quilter-Pinner, H. and Swift, D. (2017), 'Making the difference: Breaking the link between school exclusion and social exclusion', London: Institute for Public Policy Research.

Gill, T. (2010), 'Nothing ventured...: Balancing risks and benefits in the outdoors', Nottingham: English Outdoor Council.

Gillard, D. (2018), 'Education in England: A history', www.educationengland.org.uk/history/index.html

Golann, J. W. (2015), 'The paradox of success at a no-excuses school', *Sociology of Education*, 88, (2), 103–119.

Goleman, D. (2000), 'Leadership that gets results', *Harvard Business Review*, https://hbr.org/2000/03/leadership-that-gets-results

Goleman, D., Boyatzis, R. E. and McKee, A. (2013), *Primal Leadership: Unleashing the power of emotional intelligence*. Boston, MA: Harvard Business Review.

Grant, A. M. (2009), 'Coach or couch?', *Harvard Business Review*, 87, (1), 97.

HM Inspectorate of Prisons (2015), 'HM Chief Inspector of Prisons for England and Wales: Annual Report 2014–15', www.justiceinspectorates.gov.uk/hmiprisons/wp-content/uploads/sites/4/2015/07/HMIP-AR_2014-15_TSO_Final1.pdf

House of Commons Education Committee (2018), 'Forgotten children: Alternative provision and the scandal of ever increasing exclusions', London: House of Commons.

Hutchings, M. (2015), 'Exam factories? The impact of accountability measures on children and young people', London: National Union of Teachers.

Hymas, C. (2019), 'Knife crime epidemic in primary schools as figures show dozens of young children were arrested last year', *Telegraph*, www.telegraph.co.uk/news/2019/09/15/knife-crime-epidemic-primary-schools-figures-show-dozens-young

International Coach Federation (2019), 'Code of ethics', www.coachfederation.org.uk/credentialing/icf-code-of-ethics

Ipsos (2018), 'Ipsos MORI Veracity Index 2018', www.ipsos.com/sites/default/files/ct/news/documents/2018-11/veracity_index_2018_v1_161118_public.pdf

Joseph Rowntree Foundation (2018), 'UK Poverty 2018: A comprehensive analysis of poverty trends and figures', www.jrf.org.uk/report/uk-poverty-2018

Klassen, R. M., Perry, N. E. and Frenzel, A. C. (2012), 'Teachers' relatedness with students: An underemphasized component of teachers' basic psychological needs', *Journal of Educational Psychology*, 104, (1), 150–165.

Kotter, J. (1996), *Leading Change*. Boston, MA: Harvard Business School Press.

Lynch, S., Worth, J., Theobald, K. and Mills, B. (2017), 'Keeping your head: NFER analysis of headteacher retention', Slough: National Foundation for Educational Research.

Manning, E. (2017), 'Out with the old school? The rise of ed tech in the classroom', *Guardian*, www.theguardian.com/small-business-network/2017/aug/01/schools-slowly-edtech-sector-cubetto-kahoot-firefly

Marzano, R. J. (2003), *What Works in Schools: Translating research into action*. Alexandria, VA: ACSD.

Marzano, R. J., Marzano, J. S. and Pickering, D. (2003), *Classroom Management That Works: Research-based strategies for every teacher*. Alexandria, VA: ASCD.

McManus, S., Bebbington, P., Jenkins, R. and Brugha, T. (eds.), (2016), 'Mental health and wellbeing in England: Adult Psychiatric Morbidity Survey 2014', Leeds: NHS Digital.

Millard, W. Bowen-Viner, K., Baars, S., Trethewey, A. and Menzies, L. (2018), 'Boys on track: Improving support for Black Caribbean and Free School Meal-Eligible White Boys in London', London: LKMCo.

Mindell, A. (1995), *Sitting in the Fire: Large group transformation using conflict and diversity*. Florence: Deep Democracy Exchange.

NASUWT (2019), 'Government and employers failing in their duty of care to teachers and pupils', www.nasuwt.org.uk/article-listing/government-employers-failing-in-their-duty-of-care.html

National College for Teaching and Leadership, 'Developing the vision', https://apps.nationalcollege.org.uk/resources/modules/academies/academies-online-resource/ac-s3/ac-s3-t6.html

Nayar, V. (2013), 'Three differences between managers and leaders', *Harvard Business Review*, https://hbr.org/2013/08/tests-of-a-leadership-transiti

Neff, K., '*Self-compassion*', https://self-compassion.org

Obsuth, I., Murray, A. L., Malti, T., Sulger, P., Ribeaud, D. and Eisner, M. (2017), 'A non-bipartite propensity score analysis of the effects of teacher–student relationships on adolescent problem and prosocial behavior', *Journal of Youth and Adolescence*, 46, 1661–1687.

Ofcom (2018), 'Communications Market Report', London: Ofcom.

Parsloe, E. (1999), *The Manager as Coach and Mentor*. New York, NY: McGraw-Hill Education.

Poorkavoos, M. (2016), 'Compassionate leadership: What is it and why do organisations need more of it?, Horsham: Roffey Park.

Porritt, V. and Featherstone, K. (eds.), (2019), *10% Braver: Inspiring women to lead education*. London: Sage.

Power, S. (2017), 'Social media and young people', https://wiserd.ac.uk/news/social-media-and-young-people

Press Association (2018), 'Two-thirds of teachers think of quitting over bad behaviour, survey finds', *Guardian*, www.theguardian.com/education/2018/dec/16/two-thirds-of-teachers-think-of-quitting-over-bad-behaviour-survey-finds

Ratcliffe, R. (2013), 'What's the difference between leadership and management?', *Guardian*, www.theguardian.com/careers/difference-between-leadership-management

Rhodes, C. and Fletcher, S. (2013), 'Coaching and mentoring for self-efficacious leadership in schools', *International Journal of Mentoring and Coaching in Education*, 2, (1), 47–63.

Roosevelt, T. (1910), 'Citizenship in a Republic' (speech). 23 April, Sorbonne, Paris.

Scottish Government (2017), 'Included, engaged and involved part 2: Preventing and managing school exclusions', www.gov.scot/publications/included-engaged-involved-part-2-positive-approach-preventing-managing-school/pages/2

Secretary of State for Education and Employment (1997), 'Excellence in schools', London: HMSO.

Shahid, S. (2015), 'Lack of leadership', in 'Outlook on the Global Agenda 2015', pp. 14–19. Geneva: World Economic Forum.

Siddique, H. (2019), 'Impact of social media on children faces fresh scrutiny', *Guardian*, www.theguardian.com/media/2019/jan/15/impact-social-media-children-mental-health

Social Mobility Commission (2019), 'State of the Nation 2018–19: Social Mobility in Great Britain', www.gov.uk/government/publications/social-mobility-in-great-britain-state-of-the-nation-2018-to-2019

Spielman, A. (2018), 'Amanda Spielman launches Ofsted's Annual Report 2017/18', www.gov.uk/government/speeches/amanda-spielman-launches-ofsteds-annual-report-201718

Starr, J. (2011), *The Coaching Manual: The definitive guide to the process, principles and skills of personal coaching*. 3rd edn. Harlow: Pearson Education.

Staufenberg, J. (2019), 'Over 40% of "underperforming" schools improve when Progress 8 includes pupil background', *Schools Week*, https://schoolsweek.co.uk/forty-per-cent-of-secondary-schools-would-not-be-underperforming-if-pupil-background-accounted-for-research-reveals

Teacher Tapp (2019), 'Behaviour: What is going on in schools? (And how does it affect teachers?)', https://teachertapp.co.uk/behaviour-what-is-really-going-on-in-schools-2019

The School Exclusion Project (2019), 'The School Exclusion Project', https://schoolexclusionproject.com

The Trussell Trust (2019), 'Record 1.6m food bank parcels given to people in past year as the Trussell Trust calls for end to Universal Credit five week wait', www.trusselltrust.org/2019/04/25/record-1-6m-food-bank-parcels

Timpson, E. (2019), *The Timpson Review*, London: HMSO.

Tirraoro, T. (2018), 'Exclusions 2018: Children with SEND six times more likely to be excluded', *Special Needs Jungle*, www.specialneedsjungle.com/exclusions-2018-children-with-send-six-times-more-likely-to-be-excluded

Ward, H. (2018), 'Looked-after children are five times more likely to be temporarily excluded, and six other figures released today', *TES*, www.tes.com/news/looked-after-children-are-five-times-more-likely-be-temporarily-excluded-and-six-other-figures

Welsh Government (2019), 'Exclusion from schools and pupil referral units (PRU)', https://gov.wales/exclusion-schools-and-pupil-referral-units-pru

Williams, J. (2018), '"It just grinds you down": Persistent disruptive behaviour in schools and what can be done about it', London: Policy Exchange.

Worth, J. (2018), 'Latest teacher retention statistics paint a bleak picture for teacher supply in England', Slough: National Foundation for Educational Research.

Young, V. (2011), *The Secret Thoughts of Successful Women: Why capable people suffer from the impostor syndrome and how to thrive in spite of it*. New York, NY: Crown Publishing Group.

Index